They Converted Our Ancestors

A Study of the Early Church in Britain

JOHN FOSTER

Professor of Ecclesiastical History
in the University of Glasgow

SCM PRESS LTD
BLOOMSBURY STREET LONDON

FIRST PUBLISHED 1965
© SCM PRESS LTD 1965
PRINTED IN GREAT BRITAIN BY
BILLING AND SONS LIMITED
GUILDFORD AND LONDON

CONTENTS

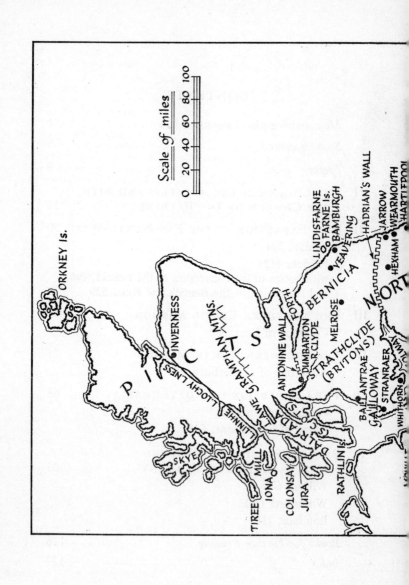

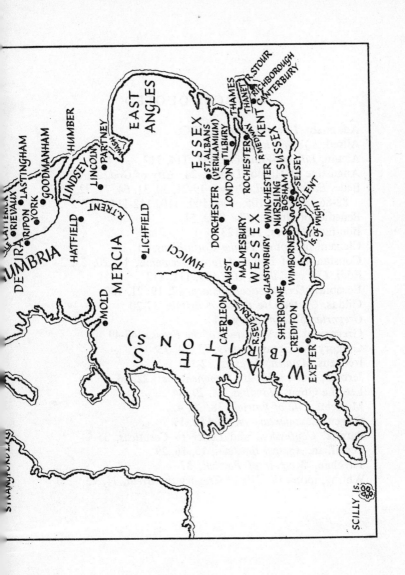

SOURCES QUOTED

Adamnan, *Life of Columba*, 52-70
Ailred, *Life of Ninian*, 31
Alcuin, *Life of Willibrord*, 111, 114, 117
Augustine of Hippo, *Letters*, 24; *City of God*, 28, 29
Bede, *Ecclesiastical History*, 19-21, 30, 31, 64, 71, 72, 75-79, 82-86, 88-102, 105, 106, 109, 110, 112-114, 117
Benedict of Nursia, *The Rule*, 51
Boniface, *Letters*, 115-123
Clement of Rome, *To the Corinthians*, 11
Constantius of Lyons, *Life of Germanus*, 17, 20, 23, 24
Eddi, *Life of Wilfrid*, 104, 109, 111, 112
Eusebius, *Ecclesiastical History*, 12, 19, 21, 106
Gildas, *On the Overthrow of Britain*, 17-20
Gregorian Sacramentary, 81
Gregory of Tours, *History of the Franks*, 47-49
Gregory the Great, *Letters*, 72, 74, 75
Irenaeus, *Against Heresies*, 12-14
Jerome, *Letters*, 25, 26; *Commentaries*, 22, 26
Leo the Great, *Homilies*, 28, 29, 44
Muirchu, *Life of Patrick*, 38, 39, 42
Origen, *Commentary on Ezekiel*, 17
Patrick, *Confession*, and *Letter to Coroticus*, 35-44
Tertullian, *Against the Jews*, 15, 16, 29
Tirechan, *Memoir of Patrick*, 37
Whitby, monk of, *Life of Gregory the Great*, 71, 72

PREFACE

CENTRAL IN Church history is the mission of the Church. One period of first importance is that immediately beyond the New Testament. Having contributed *After the Apostles: Missionary Preaching of the first three centuries*, it seemed natural to turn to the Early Church of one's own land. Again the interest is in missionaries at work.

A small book on a big subject must select. The principle of selection has been to work directly from the most reliable sources, and to linger longest where we can see, and share with, those who brought the Christian faith to our ancestors.

Translation of Patrick, Bede, Adamnan, and most other primary sources, is my own. I hope it may give to the reader some fraction of the joy which it has given to me. Especially have I rejoiced in the Venerable Bede. If the book were more worthy, I should dedicate it to him. Instead, I will add here at the beginning his own final prayer.

And now, good Jesus, grant that I,
to whom Thy grace hath given this sweet drink of knowledge,
may, in Thine own good time, come to Thee, the very fount of wisdom,
and ever stand before Thy face.

Easter 1964

JOHN FOSTER

I

The Link with the Apostles
and with the Church of the Fathers

MANY HAVE sought for the Church in Britain an apostolic
founder. Two claims deserve notice, one because its evidence is as early as AD 95, the other because it is widely
known through literature and art.

St Clement of Rome, a younger contemporary of the
Apostles, writes this of St Paul:

> He taught the whole world righteousness, came to the limit
> of the west, bore witness before the rulers, and so passed
> from this world and was received up into the holy place,
> becoming the greatest pattern of endurance.[1]

'The limit of the west'—why should this not mean our
distant isle?

There are two reasons why not. First, St Paul, some forty
years before, had told this church in Rome that he intended,
after visiting them, to go on to Spain (Rom. 15.24, 28).
Clement seems to be stating that he did so. And second, any
one writing from Rome about 'the limit of the west' would
most naturally mean the Mediterranean's western extremity,
the Straits of Gibraltar.

A second more appealing story tells that St Philip sent
Joseph of Arimathaea with twelve companions, bringing the
holy grail and the thorn which still flowers at Glastonbury.
This legend provides material for poet and artist, but the
historian must look askance at it. William of Malmesbury
(c. 1080-1143) is the earliest writer to record it. It is evidence
of nothing more than the statement with which we began,
about desire for an apostolic founder. And none in Britain
had more right to such imaginings than the monks of the

[1] *Clement to the Corinthians*, 5.

pre-Saxon monastery at Glastonbury. Malmesbury is only forty miles away.

Instead of using these questionable devices, twisting the natural meaning of geography, using legends to fabricate a history, let me lead you from the Apostles to the earliest Church in Britain, using history all the way.

The Apostle on whom we must fix our eyes is St John. Irenaeus, Bishop of Lyons, writing in the year 185, says,

> The church in Ephesus was founded by Paul, and there John lived till the time of Trajan,[1]

which means 'till AD 98'. Irenaeus was a disciple of Polycarp, Bishop of Smyrna, who was a disciple of St John. This is what Irenaeus says:

> I remember things then better than those which happened recently. For lessons of boyhood grow up with the mind and become a part of it. So I am able to speak even of the place where the blessed Polycarp sat and discoursed, his goings and comings, the manner of his life, his physical appearance, his discourses to the people. He used to talk away of his intercourse with John, and with the rest of those who had seen the Lord. He would recall their sayings, and this and that which he had heard from them about the Lord, about his mighty works, and his teaching. . . . These things even then, since the mercy of God was upon me, I used to listen to eagerly, noting them for remembrance not on paper but in my very heart. And ever since, by God's grace, I literally go ruminating upon them.[2]

So for Irenaeus, as well as for the aged Polycarp, Smyrna was a church of apostolic association. We may recall that, of the seven churches in the opening chapters of the Revelation, Smyrna stands second, after St John's own Ephesus. The service of the Church was to call Irenaeus to a very different scene. After a period in Rome, he was sent to Gaul. In Gaul there were Greek colonies, some of them older than the Roman province, and still maintaining strong connec-

[1] *Against Heresies*, III, 3.
[2] Quoted by Eusebius, *Ecclesiastical History*, V, 20.

tions with the east. It was through such connections that the Christian faith had reached them, and that Irenaeus now came as presbyter to the congregation at Lyons. When in the year 177 persecution struck this church, and the one linked to it at Vienne, twenty miles to the south, survivors wrote an account of the forty-eight martyrs, for 'the brethren in Asia and Phrygia', and the church historian Eusebius has passed it on to us. Irenaeus escaped because he happened to be at Rome on the church's business. On his return he was made bishop of the ravaged and scattered flock. It is with him that we notice an extension of the church's outreach.

Among the forty-eight martyrs are some whose names indicate Greek colonial descent; others, of whatever race, have Latin names. From Irenaeus, however, we hear of natives, Celts, won to the faith. Years ago I gave a series of fifty radio talks, called *What are the Churches Doing?* I overheard my producer say, 'Whatever he's talking about, he always seems to bring in China.' That was the result of missionary experience, the memorable experience of crossing the barrier of language and being at home in a different culture. Irenaeus seems to feel like this about the Celts.

He begins his great work *Against Heresies* by telling his readers not to expect anything pretentious; his writing will be plain matter-of-fact.

> We spend our days among the Celts, and are busy for the most part with a barbarous language. So you will not look to us for a skill in words which we have not acquired, nor for ability in writing which we have not practised, nor for adornments of style and persuasiveness to which we are strangers.

His theme is that the Christian faith is one and the same throughout the world. In illustrating it he says,

> The churches planted in Germany do not believe or pass on anything different, nor those in Spain, nor those among the Celts.[1]

[1] *Against Heresies*, I, 10.

He claims that the apostolic tradition is known, and adds that this is so, even apart from the apostolic writings:

> Many barbarous peoples believe in Christ. They have not a sheet of paper, nor a drop of ink, but they do have salvation written by the Spirit in their hearts, and they carefully guard the ancient tradition. . . . Without letters, they have believed this Faith, barbarians as to language, but wise indeed as to doctrine and manner of life. . . . Let any one preach these made-up heresies, and they will at once stop up their ears and run far away.[1]

Irenaeus is again thinking of his Celtic converts. The only writing which survives borrows Greek letters in the south, and Latin in the north, for writing Gaulish sounds. Most would not read or write at all.

Irenaeus, in opposing heresy, was for ever pointing back to the Apostles. For us, he stands as our best link with the Apostles. For consider: St John in Palestine had been the Lord's disciple. Polycarp in Ephesus had been St John's disciple. Irenaeus in Smyrna had been Polycarp's disciple. And Irenaeus left Greek-speaking Smyrna for the Latin-speaking west, and learned a Celtic language as missionary in Gaul, with our own islands, also Celtic-speaking, just across the Channel. And if you feel that, by the time it reaches us, the link is too indirect, hear again from Irenaeus:

> This preaching and this Faith, received from the Apostles, the Church, though scattered over the whole world, guards as if it lived in one house, believes as if it had but one mind, preaches, teaches and hands on as if it had but one mouth. And although there are different languages in the world, the force of the tradition is one and the same.

Here is our link with the Apostles. It is likely that before Irenaeus had finished his course, about the year 200, the faith was planted in our islands.

[1] Op. cit., III, 4.

In the period between 200 and 206, Tertullian of Carthage wrote his book *Against the Jews*. In its seventh section we first hear of Christians in Britain. This evidence Harnack dismisses brusquely, 'Tertullian's notice is of no consequence.'[1] I do not see why. Tertullian quotes Psalm 19.4,

> Their line is gone out through all the earth,
> and their words to the end of the world.

And he asks,

> In whom have all the nations believed but in Christ who has already come?

Then follows his list of nations among whom Christians are to be found. He begins,

> Parthians and Medes and Elamites and the dwellers in Mesopotamia.

This is to be expected. Tertullian was a Latin belonging to Carthage. The main body of the second-century Church was Greek, around the eastern half of the Mediterranean. Beyond these, further into Asia, were Christians whose language was Syriac. Here was a gap in his knowledge. So he fills in by quoting Acts 2.9, places from which came some of the converts on the day of Pentecost. From the Church's eastern extremity, he next turns to the western end,

> And there are other nations, such as the various kinds of Getuli, and the many territories of the Mauri.

Detail now, because he is near home—the tribes bordering the Sahara, and the Moors nearer the coast. From North Africa he crosses the Straits.

> And all the boundaries of Spain.

That was known too. Spain was on the list from St Paul's own day (Romans 15.24, 28, and Clement to the Corinthians 5, quoted on p. 11). He continues, 'The different peoples of Gaul'. He must have had personal knowledge

[1] *Mission and Expansion of Christianity*, II, 272.

here. The forty-eight martyrs of Lyons had been famous for twenty-five years, and the equally famous Irenaeus, Bishop of Lyons, was living and writing still, a man after Tertullian's own heart.

And next he mentions, 'places of the Britons'. Why assume that suddenly he is entering the unknown, leaving fact for fiction? As if to reassure us Tertullian gives more than the geographical reference. He writes,

> Places of the Britons, unreached by the Romans, but subject to Christ.

Such a man as Tertullian would know of Hadrian's Wall, built in AD 128. He would know too of the attempt that the later Antonine Wall represents, to hold the Forth and the Clyde as civilization's frontier. A few years before Tertullian wrote, in 196, the governor of Britain had rebelled against the Emperor Septimius Severus and moved his troops into Gaul. The northern tribes rose, broke through the Antonine Wall, and ravaged as far south as York. In the years that followed Hadrian's Wall had had to be rebuilt. In 206 the new governor of Britain called for a campaign to re-establish the Forth-Clyde line—the last campaign of Septimius Severus, who was to die at York in 211. This is the very period, 200-206, of Tertullian's writing. Whichever the actual year, Britain was in the news. Tertullian, living in Carthage, was almost as near the centre of the Empire as in Italy itself. And in the midst of these events Tertullian is claiming that the Church reaches farther than the might of Rome. His enthusiasm may have carried him away; he often does exaggerate. But one cannot easily say that he had no facts to go on.

To this reference we must add one made, probably between 238 and 240, by Origen. Unlike the Latin Tertullian, Origen belonged to the Greek eastern end of the Mediterranean, teaching first in his native Alexandria and, after 231, in Palestinian Caesarea. But he travelled widely, visiting Rome, for example, as a young man, before 218, and writing the work about to be quoted during a second visit to Athens.[1] Wherever he went, he kept ears and eyes open, and drank in all that was to be learned. In a context similar to that of Tertullian's statement, claiming that Old Testament prophecy is fulfilled in the universal spread of Christianity, and in that alone, he writes in his commentary on Ezekiel:

> When, until the coming of Christ, did the land of Britain accept belief in one God? Or the Moors of Africa? Or the whole globe? But now there are churches on the frontiers of the world, and all the earth shouts for joy to the God of Israel.

He mentions Christians in Britain similarly in two other passages.

Next in order of time comes Albanus the martyr, about the year 303. The biographer of St Germanus, Bishop of Auxerre in Gaul, writing about 480, is the first to mention his shrine. Germanus came (as we shall see) on a mission of help in 429, and before returning,

> made his way to the blessed Albanus the martyr, to give thanks to God through him.

Who was he?

Haddan's article in the *Dictionary of Christian Biography* begins, 'Albanus, the protomartyr of Britain—if he ever existed'—which is hardly encouraging. For details of place, estimate of the time, and a story of the martyrdom, we have to go on to Gildas, a monk who about the year 560 wrote the history of his country's ruin by the heathen English. Before getting to that sad story of his own times, he reviews the heroic period of persecution under the Emperor Diocletian, in the years following 303:

> God, who willeth that all men should be saved, did not leave Britain full-shrouded in the thick darkness of black night. In the above-mentioned persecution, as we infer, he lit for us the brightest of lights. And the graves of their bones, and the

[1] According to Eusebius, *Ecclesiastical History*, VI, 33.

places of their martyrdom, might now in the minds of beholders excite no small fervour of love to God, had they not, in return for our exceeding wickedness, been lost to our people by the lamentable disruption of the barbarians. I mean Albanus of Verulamium, Aaron and Julius, citizens of the City of the Legions, and others of both sexes and in different places, who stood fast with the highest courage in the contest for Christ. The first of these . . . for the sake of love, saved another confessor when he was about to be taken, by hiding him in his house and then changing clothes with him. In this he followed the example of Christ, who laid down his life for his sheep.[1]

'City of the Legions' means 'garrison town', and might be used of several places. Probably *urbs legionum* here means Caerleon in Monmouthshire, that very name being a telescoping of *castra legionum*. More decisive, the charter of a church dedicated to 'the holy martyrs, Julius and Aaron' can be traced in Caerleon back to about the year 870.[2] One hears of none other such, and probably this dedication goes back to the time of Gildas, three centuries before. Gildas speaks of 'Albanus of Verulamium'. Again, no other town claims him.

Just one thing might make us doubt the geography. Among the marvels which Gildas records as Albanus went to his death is this:

He opened a path across the noble river Thames, whose waters stood abrupt like cliffs on either hand.

Verulamium (St Albans) has a small stream which flows into a tributary of the Thames, but it could hardly be called a noble river, and its waters, if divided, would not make cliffs. Still, we need not doubt. Gildas depends on an earlier martyr-story. His knowledge of the place is hearsay. There is no doubt that at a shrine here Bishop Germanus gave thanks in the year 430, and that this was the scene of Albanus's martyrdom.

[1] *On the Overthrow of Britain*, 10.
[2] According to Hugh Williams, *Christianity in Early Britain*, 105.

But when? You would notice Gildas's qualifying clause, 'as we infer'. He did not know, so how can we? Some indeed have challenged his inference, and on this ground: Eusebius emphatically states that Constantius Chlorus, the western Caesar and later Augustus, under whose rule Britain lay, 'was favourable and kind. He took not the smallest part in the persecution of Christians'.[1] Must we say that Albanus and Aaron and Julius, and the others of both sexes, go back beyond Diocletian's persecution in 303, to Valerian in 260, or Decius in 250? Three considerations make me say No. First, Eusebius is writing in the pro-Christian reign of Constantius's son, Constantine. What more natural than to exaggerate the peace of the Church under Constantine's father? Second, apart from such exaggeration, Eusebius's words need not mean that there were no local incidents, no underlings who persecuted, when persecution was the declared imperial policy. And third, I cannot recall ever having had to rescue a personage of the Early Church from too late a date: a historian's work moves in the opposite direction.

Here then we have found a real saint, a fixed place, a probable date—Albanus, Verulamium, soon after 303. Now, what of the story of the martyrdom? Gildas gives some of it, but the fullest account is in Bede's *Ecclesiastical History of the English People*, I, 7—a book which was written in 731. We may thus seem to be turning to a record which, compared with Gildas's 560, is very late. However, Bede's section on Albanus has long been recognized as of different style, a unit complete in itself. Gildas depended on an earlier martyr-story, but Bede seems to have lifted the story as it stood and incorporated it in his text. This was suspected before. In the year 1904 it was proved by Professor Wilhelm Meyer of Göttingen in a fine example of modern historical and literary criticism.[2] Meyer discovered

---

[1] *Ecclesiastical History*, VIII, 13; still more fulsome praise in *Life of Constantine*, 13-18.
[2] W. Levison, in *Antiquity*, 1941, pp. 337-59.

manuscripts of this *Passio Albani*. It survives in three recensions, first the martyr-story, second an epitome of it, third a re-expansion of the epitome. It was this third which Bede, and to a less extent Gildas, used. So the first recension cannot be much later than 500. There are signs that it was composed in Auxerre. Constantius of Lyons wrote his *Life of Germanus* about the year 480, mentioning (as we have seen) the shrine of St Albanus, whom nobody knew. Who was this martyr of Britain, so revered by their own great Bishop?

But if no one at Auxerre knew about Albanus, how could anyone there write about his martyrdom? Meyer's detailed work on this *Passio Albani* shows that they borrowed extracts from a number of Roman and Gallic martyrologies—a happening belonging to this saint, a conversation attributed to that, a miracle after the manner of still another. Sometimes the very phrasing is retained, and all are transferred to St Albanus. Let me outline the story which results:

Albanus, a heathen, gives shelter to a Christian priest. His example, and then his instruction, win Albanus to the faith. Soldiers come to arrest the priest, but Albanus wears his cloak, and gets himself taken. The judge demands his name, but Albanus is more concerned to confess his faith. The judge commands him to sacrifice to the gods. Albanus says they are not gods but devils. He is condemned. Crowds coming to watch the execution fill the river bridge. So Albanus, eager for martyrdom, goes to the riverside, and the water dries up for him to cross. At this the executioner throws down his sword and is converted. On the hilltop an opposite miracle is performed. Albanus prays for water, and a spring rises close by. Then both Albanus and his convert are beheaded. Here we must quote from Bede:

On the twenty-second day of June, near to the city of Verulamium, which by the English is now called Verlamacaestir or Vaeclingacaestir.

This last is the name that we also find in '*Watling* Street'. Bede continues,

> And here when the peace of Christian times returned, a church was built of wonderful workmanship, worthy of this martyr. And in it truly, even to this day, there are ceaselessly fulfilled the healing of the sick and a continuance of good works.

This addition of Bede's is history, but we may well feel impatient with the made-up items which went before. No, our protomartyr has not much of a history. And yet there are things to think about, and preach about, on or near his festival on the 22nd of June. The details of the story have no value as history, but they have a typological value, expressing general truths. Let me mention four such.

First, the river made way for the saint to cross. To the Christian, death is the crossing of the Jordan to the promised land.

Second, the spring bubbled up at the place of execution. For the man who prays, the water of God's comfort is there in the midst of suffering.

Third, the executioner was himself converted. That is true to the martyr tradition. 'Martyr' is 'witness', and it is this witness which prevails. As Tertullian has said, 'The blood of Christians is seed.'

And last, also true to tradition is that conflict of Albanus with his judge, when he tells him that his name and family do not matter. The records of the forty-eight martyrs of Lyons in the year 177 are eye-witness accounts, and of one of them it is said,

> He did not tell his own name, nor race, nor city, nor whether he were slave or free, but to all their questions he returned answer in the Latin language, *Christianus sum.*

Yes, that is all that matters.

With what Bede calls 'the peace of Christian times', we come to the Synod of Arles, 314. The Emperor Constantine, newly embarked on his pro-Christian policy, wished to see the Church contribute to the unity of the

Empire, and lo, in North Africa the unity of the Church itself was threatened. One party refused to recognize Caecilian as Bishop of Carthage, because they suspected that the Bishop who had consecrated him had given in, in the final persecutions. They set up a rival Bishop, Donatus. The Emperor instructed the bishops of the west to meet at Arles and settle their differences with these Donatists. Among the thirty-three who came were three from Britain, who are thus styled:

> *Eborius Episcopus de civitate Eboracensi provincia Britannia,*
> *Restitutus Episcopus de civitate Londinensi provincia suprascripta,*
> *Adelfius Episcopus de civitate Colonia Londinensium.*

Here at last is evidence about which we have no doubts at all, except with regard to one of the places. The first bishop belongs to York. His name may be the one more usually written 'Ebur' or 'Ivor', its Latinization here being influenced by the place-name, Eboracum. The second is of London. The third can hardly be of London also. The pen of some scribe must have repeated the *Londinensi* above (with the addition of *-um*), instead of some similar name. The emendation requiring least change is *Colonia Lindensium*, 'the colony of the people of Lindsey, i.e. Lincoln'.

But if in 314 we have three undoubted names, they are names and nothing more. For a known person we have to go on to about the year 400. And then there comes this blow to our insular pride: the first Christian from Britain who is a vital figure in church history is the heretic Pelagius. Where did he come from? Pelagius is Latinized Greek, 'man of the sea'. The true Latin would be 'Marinus'. Some have recognized him as a Welshman called Morgan, which means 'born of the sea'. The contemporary Jerome makes him more barbarous still. He writes,

> He has his lineage of Scottish race from the neighbourhood of the Britons,[1]

thus placing him in Ireland. In controversy Jerome always tried to make his opponent look ridiculous, and he goes on

[1] Prologue to the *Commentary on Jeremiah*.

to describe Pelagius as *pultibus Scottorum praegravatus*, 'weighed down with the porridge of the Scots', surely literature's first reference to that national dish. Pelagius's heresy was well intentioned. He was concerned about lack of moral effort among Christians in Rome, and thought that it was due to their acceptance of the doctrine of original sin, a fallen nature inherited from Adam. What man needed, he said, was not radical transformation by the grace of God, but just to be taught better, and himself to make the effort to be better. From Rome Pelagius passed on to Sicily in 409, then on again to North Africa, with the crowds of displaced persons fleeing before the barbarian invasion. Rome fell to Alaric and his Visigoths in 410. Pelagius is unheard of after 418. Probably he died in Palestine. Though he himself never returned to Britain, his teaching did come to trouble the Church there. A synod invited two bishops of Gaul to come over as a mission of help, Germanus of Auxerre and Lupus of Troyes, and in the year 429 they came.

The biographer of Germanus gives us a glimpse of Britain in the brief interval between the departure of the Romans and the settlement of the English. With the Roman legions had gone the Roman peace. The Picts were ravaging from the north, and already Saxons were raiding from over the North Sea. The two bishops went to work vigorously. They preached as they travelled through the country, sometimes in the little churches, often to greater numbers out-of-doors. Finally they met the Pelagian leaders in a full-scale debate, and the crowd, too great for any building, acclaimed the bishops with shouts of victory. The biographer continues:

> Thus the damnable heresy of Pelagius was put down, its agents were silenced and the souls of all were settled in purity of faith.

It is here that he mentions the bishops' going to St Albanus's shrine, and adds,

The special merits and mediation of Albanus the martyr, afforded them a calm crossing [of the Channel], and in quietness the happy vessel brought back the great men to their waiting people.

But between the accomplishment of their mission and their return home, Germanus had given help of another kind. Before his sudden and surprising consecration as bishop in 418, he had been a high-ranking official of the Empire, with more experience of political and military than of church affairs. A small British army, soon to meet massed Pictish and Saxon invaders, besought his help. The two bishops are said to have won many converts among the non-Christian soldiers, given them their first instruction, and on Easter Eve brought them to baptism. Then Bishop Germanus took over the command. He deployed his small force in a narrow glen, as if for an ambush. As the enemy approached, the bishops raised again the Easter greeting, a threefold 'Alleluia!' The Britons with one voice responded, 'Alleluia!' The cry echoed and re-echoed through the defile, and the heathen fled in terror, without a blow. A place called Maes-Garmon, just outside Mold in Flintshire, may well be 'field of Germanus', the scene of this 'Alleluia Victory'. Germanus made a second visit in 447, accompanied this time by Bishop Severus of Treves. He died in the following year.

We must next turn to Ninian and Patrick, close together in time, and probably in place, and of far greater importance than any Christian predecessors in Britain, because they stand at the beginning of a period of new Christian expansion. That may seem a strange statement about such a time. For history counts the fifth century as the end of the long period of Graeco-Roman civilization, and, in church history, the end of the Church of the Fathers. As for beginnings, we call the next five centuries the Dark Ages. Already we have noticed a shadow coming over the sky—in 409 'displaced persons fleeing before barbarian invasion', and in 429 Britain invaded by heathen Picts and Saxons. The 'Alleluiah Victory' was only a brief respite. As the title of Gildas's book indicates, the heathen did accomplish the overthrow of Britain. We are at the end of an age.

True, some historians have protested against this interpretation of the fifth century, pointing out that life was not lived under a sense of crisis, that even the dramatic fall of Rome in 410 lasted only three days, and was not seen by most as the final calamity.

But for the more far-seeing, catastrophe was here. In the writing of Jerome and Augustine doom is sounded.

Jerome (342-420) was foremost among advocates of monasticism in the west. His choice of the other-worldly way was not unconnected with flight from a world which was falling before the barbarians. From youth to age, such happenings form the background to his life. In 376, when he was thirty, there came news that the Goths had overrun his home town, Stridon in Dalmatia. Relatives were dead, and family property reduced to a cluster of ruins. Years afterwards he mentions selling the land on which the ruins stood, to relieve refugees from a later barbarian invasion.

He refers back to this tragedy of 376 in a letter dated 396:

> I shudder to think of the catastrophes of our time. For more than twenty years Roman blood has daily been shed, from Constantinople to the Julian Alps [north of the Adriatic]. The Roman world is falling, yet we hold up our heads instead of bowing them down. . . . The East indeed seemed safe, but in the last year wolves were let loose upon us [in Bethlehem] from the Caucasus [the Huns]. . . . It is our sins which make the barbarians strong, our vices which overcome Rome's soldiers. . . . If only I had a watch-tower so high as to view the whole earth, I would show you the wreck of a world.

In 409 he wrote,

> While I am talking about the cargo, the vessel itself is sinking. 'The one that restraineth' is being 'taken out of the way' (II

Thess. 2.7). . . . Anti-Christ is near. . . . Savage tribes in countless numbers have overrun the whole of Gaul. From the Alps
to the Pyrenees, from the Rhine to the Atlantic, all has been
laid waste. . . . And whom the sword from without spares,
famine ravages within. . . . I cannot speak without tears.

In 410 came the news to Bethlehem that Alaric and his
Visigoths had taken Rome. For years afterwards, Jerome
keeps recalling how he felt when he heard it. In a letter
dated 412 he says,

A dreadful rumour came from the west. Rome had been
sacked. My tongue cleaves to the roof of my mouth, and my
voice is choked with sobs to think that that city is captive
which led captive the whole world.

And again in 413,

The whole world sinks into ruin. Aye, but to our shame our
sins live on and thrive. The great city, capital of the Empire,
is devoured in one huge fire, and never a part of the earth
where there are not Roman refugees.

In 414, the introduction to his commentary on Ezekiel
explains why the work is so long overdue:

The light was put out. The Empire was beheaded. The whole
world died with the one city. . . .
Who would have believed that Rome, grown great by conquest
of the world, would fall, the mother of nations would become
their tomb? . . . There is no hour, almost no single moment,
when we are not relieving crowds of refugees, and the quiet of
the monastery has turned into the bustle of a guest-house. So
much so that we had either to shut our doors on them or aban-
don our study of the Scriptures. . . . I am not boasting, as
some may suspect, of the welcome given to the fugitives, but
just acknowledging the causes of delay. . . . We did give up the
exposition of Ezekiel, and almost all study, and were filled
with a longing to turn the words of Scripture into deeds, not
just saying holy things but doing them. . . . In addition to
these hindrances, my eyes are growing dim with age.

He was then seventy-two. Poor Jerome! He had fled from
a falling world to give himself to the Word of God which

abideth for ever, and then, like the good monk he was, he turned even from the Word of God, to practise that charity which the Word enjoins. In both renunciations he was preparing for the future. His Latin Vulgate was to be the Bible for the West, through the Dark Ages and the Middle Ages. And the monastery, where men lived who had renounced the world, continued through troublous times as a haven, a refuge, a little centre of civilized living where the pen was wielded and not the sword, and a quiet preparation for a Christian future.

The tragedy of the year 410 struck Augustine in a different way. The young Proconsul of the North African province, Volusianus, was preparing for Christian baptism when he heard of the fall of Rome. He raised two questions inevitable to such a crisis. First, the pacifist question. Can a Christian, *ought* a Christian if he is responsible for a Roman province, to obey literally the teaching, 'Recompense no man evil for evil', 'Whosoever smiteth thee on thy right cheek turn to him the other also'? And second, the question of Providence. He put this brutally, remembering Constantine's entry of Rome in 312, and Alaric's almost exactly one century later.

> Great calamities have befallen the Commonwealth, under the rule of Emperors observing for the most part the Christian religion.

Augustine exclaimed, 'This sweeping accusation is a calumny.' His letter in reply he was to develop through thirteen years (313-326) into his greatest work, for Christians of succeeding ages *the* philosophy of history, *The City of God*. During those thirteen years the world situation was growing not better but worse. Within four years of the book's completion, he died in Hippo,[1] the barbarian flood by then having reached the city's gates. The Vandals were besieging it. Thus Augustine knew that he wrote at the end of an age, knew that he looked into darkness ahead.

[1] Today, Bone on the Algerian coast.

Sir Ernest Barker well describes his work as 'standing on the confines of two worlds, the classical and the Christian, and pointing the way forward into the Christian'.[1] At its heart is the contrast between 'the earthly city which shall not be everlasting'—the Roman Empire, or any subsequent social order which may contain the Church for a time—and the Church itself, the colony on earth of the heavenly Jerusalem, which is the City of God. The Church, on pilgrimage through history, is that which gives significance to history itself, looking for its consummation beyond history.

> Even now is the Church the Kingdom of Christ, and the Kingdom of Heaven. Even now his saints reign with him, but not as then they shall reign.

Augustine's conception of 'the two cities', often misunderstood or misapplied, influences most thinking, and much practice, concerning Church and state in both Dark Ages and Middle Ages, while the modern age too would recognize Augustine as the greatest single contributor to the doctrine of the Church since St Paul. No wonder that St Jerome and St Augustine have been hailed as 'makers of Latin Christianity'.

There is one more voice to which we must listen concerning a future beyond this century of breakdown, not that of a monk and scholar like Jerome, nor of philosopher and theologian like Augustine, but of one called to rule this Church of the West. When Augustine had been busy for some five years upon his *City of God*, he came to know a young acolyte from Rome who was used as letter-carrier between Italian and North African bishops. His name was Leo, and in the year 440 he was to become Pope. In a sermon preached on the festival of Saints Peter and Paul, June 29, Leo addressed the City thus:

> These are they who raised you to such glory that you were made a holy nation, a chosen people, a priestly and royal state (I

[1] Introduction to *The City of God*, 2 vols., Everyman's Library.

Peter 2.9), and head of the world through the blessed Peter's holy See, and so attained a wider sway by the worship of God than by earthly government. For although you were increased by many victories, and extended your rule on land and sea, yet what your toils in war subdued is less than what the peace of Christ has conquered.

These are high-sounding words for a time when the decline of the Roman Empire was advanced by one more generation. Compared with Jerome and Augustine, Leo had to face not one Fall of Rome but two. Yet, even in this respect there was a change of spirit. Leo did not write a lament for the fall of the city, nor an apology to explain God's permitting it. Leo did his utmost to save it from falling. In 452 at the approach of Attila the Hun, the distracted Romans looked to their Bishop to save them, and did not look in vain. In 455 with Gaiseric and his Vandals at Rome's ill-defended gates, the courageous Bishop led his clergy out to mediate, and place some limit on the horrors that must follow.

We saw that Tertullian was the first to claim that there were Christians in Britain, 'Places of the Britons, unreached by the Romans. . . .' For verification of this greater claim by Pope Leo, that the Church has a wider sway than the Roman Empire ever had, we must, strangely enough, turn to our own obscure island. Pope Leo died in 461. This was also the year of the death of Patrick. With Ninian and Patrick are the small beginnings of this new Christian expansion in the far north-west.

II

New Expansion in the Far North-West

NINIAN, 394 PATRICK, 432

THE DICTIONARY of Christian Biography calls St Ninian 'the first and greatest of the ancient British missionaries'. Alas that, compared with his contemporary, the heretic Pelagius, we know so little about him. Our main source is Bede's *Ecclesiastical History of the English Nation*, written in 731, and in this part of it Bede somewhat confusingly writes history backwards. He is dealing with the coming of St Aidan from Iona to Northumbria in 635. That reminds him to add a chapter on St Columba's coming to Iona seventy years before. And then he has to insert a paragraph about St Ninian, earlier again by a century and a half.

> The Southern Picts, who live on this side of the mountains [i.e. south of the Grampians], had, it is said, long before left the error of idolatry for the true faith, through the preaching of Ninian, a most reverend Bishop and holy man of the nation of the Britons, who had been regularly instructed at Rome in the faith and mysteries of the truth. His See, made famous by the name and the church of Martin Saint and Bishop, where Ninian himself, with many other Saints, lies buried, is now held by the English. The place [now] belongs to the province of the Bernicians, and is commonly called The White House (*Candida Casa*), because he built the church of stone in a manner unaccustomed to the Britons.[1]

Bede says 'regularly instructed at Rome' to make it clear that Ninian had none of the peculiar ways of Celtic monks of a later date (p. 105).

Twice Bede recounts stories told him by Pecthelm. He was a disciple of Aldhelm, Abbot of Malmesbury, who was sent to Whithorn when, in Bede's words,

[1] *Ecclesiastical History*, III, 4.

the number of the faithful had been multiplied, and it had [again] been made an episcopal see, with him as first to hold it.

This was in 730, while Bede was at work on his history. Pecthelm must have visited Bede at the monastery at Jarrow soon after coming north. So we may assume that Bede's record about Ninian represents the Whithorn tradition in 730. And this paragraph is almost all that we know. All that has been written about Ninian from then till now may be called 'variations on a theme of Bede'. The first such writer to be worthy of note is Ailred, Abbot of Rievaulx, in the twelfth century. He claims also to have an earlier Life of Ninian 'written in barbarian language', which phrase usually means 'not in Latin', but here may mean 'in bad Latin'. Whatever the value of this other source, its additions to what Bede tells us are these: Ninian's father was a chieftain in the Solway region, and a Christian. The companion of his journey was 'a brother named Plebia'. At Rome Ninian was consecrated Bishop in 394. When returning through Gaul, he stayed with St Martin at Tours. Masons from Tours built his unusual church. While it was being built, there came news of Martin's death (397). Tuduvallus, the local ruler, was converted by Ninian.

However, we have recently come to know a little more on two points, Ninian's church, and the extent of Ninian's influence. *Candida Casa*, 'White House', is now represented by the name Whithorn. But which? A village on the coast is called Isle of Whithorn, and the town of Whithorn is three miles inland. Both have ruins of ancient churches. Until recently opinion was divided as to which was *Candida Casa*. In 1949 Dr Ralegh Radford answered the question.[1] At the Isle, the ruin is a rectangular chapel 37×22 feet, mainly thirteenth century. Digging disclosed twelfth-century foundations but nothing earlier. The ruins at Whithorn are of monastic buildings including a cruciform church 250 feet long, dating from the twelfth century

[1] *Dumfries and Galloway Natural History and Archaeological Society's* 'Ninian' Volume.

onwards. Dr Radford decided to dig at the east end, because he guessed that builders of a new and bigger church would leave the altar and shrine of the old one as long as possible undisturbed. Then, as the new building advanced from the west, ready to enclose altar and shrine, the old walls would be pulled down, but their foundations might remain. Sure enough, the trenches dug disclosed foundations of a building far more ancient. Fifteen feet wide, it projects eastwards fourteen feet beyond the east window of the later priory. These oldest walls were 3 feet 4 inches thick, and built of rough undressed stones without mortar.

How does this fit Bede's description? This crude unmortared stonework, so far from being 'in a manner unaccustomed to the Britains', is typical of Celtic building as we know it in Wales and Cornwall. And the name 'White House' seems inappropriate to these dark grey Galloway shales and slates. However, on the outer face of this dry-stone walling, Dr Radford found patches of whitish mortar. He quotes this description of a later builder in North Wales, 'He made the country glitter with lime-washed churches, like the firmament with stars', and suggests that Ninian's church was so whitened. To Britons of these parts, this was a new style—hence the name, *Candida Casa*.

From the Isle of Whithorn three miles westward along the coast is St Ninian's cave. One scrambles up from the shore over a mass of boulders, then through the mouth, to descend sharply into a cave twenty-seven feet long. Dr Radford excavated this to its original depth, revealing under sand and silt many crosses, some Celtic, some Latin, carved on the rock face. It is reasonable to accept that in the Isle of Whithorn we have the scene of St Ninian's landing, in Whithorn the site of his monastery, and in the cave the place of retreat so often deemed necessary by the monk. Knowledge about Ninian has advanced in one other way, by gathering clues as to the extent of his influence. Let me begin with one discovery, not because it is important, but because it is one in which I shared. In 1957 I heard that a farmer above Ballintrae, repairing the dry-stone wall of one of his fields, had found among the topstones one which bore a roughly incised cross. This kind of detective work is the spice of an historian's life, so I went down to see. I judged it to be part of the headstone of an ancient grave. From what consecrated ground could it have come? The map showed a small loch named Kilantringan one mile to the east, and 'Ringan' is a common corruption of 'Ninian' in place-names. The loch proved to be artificial, made by damming a burn, little more than a century ago, so where did the name come from? The archaeological division of Ordnance Survey[1] produced evidence for a hamlet of that name beside the burn, on what is now just a grassy knoll. Aerial photographs have not so far produced traces of a chapel, but such there must have been. 'Kil-ant-ringan' stands for *cella sancti Niniani*, 'chapel of St Ninian'. Crude work like this gravestone is hard to date. It may be a thousand years old. It is one more place where Ninian was revered.

Churches dedicated to St Ninian, or, after the example of *Candida Casa*, to St Martin, or place-names witnessing to such dedications, may fairly be claimed as evidence of St Ninian's influence. The foremost collector and interpreter of such evidence is Dr W. D. Simpson, in *St Ninian and the Origins of the Church in Scotland*. He has shown that the influence is by no means limited, as Bede might seem to imply, to the region between the Solway and the Grampians. It goes east to Hadrian's Wall[2], and follows the line of Roman communications northwards into Aberdeenshire, Inverness, Sutherland, and even to the Northern Isles. In 1958 archaeologists from the University of Aberdeen unearthed treasure far more important than my Ballintrae cross, and this was in St Ninian's Isle, Shetland. This of course is not to claim an area of missionary work so wide for Ninian himself, nor for his immediate disciples. But it

[1] By the kindness of Mr A. L. F. Rivet.
[2] An ancient church, St Martin's, stands in farmland one mile east of Brampton.

B

does mean that people over so wide an area have looked to Ninian as their apostle—yes, 'the first and greatest of the ancient British missionaries'.

In a village called Kirkmadrine, on that last peninsula (the Rinns) of Galloway, reaching out to the Irish Sea, there is a graveyard with three Latin gravestones. The oldest Christian relics in Scotland, they go back towards, if not to, Ninian's time. One stood for years as gatepost to the graveyard. Fortunately the bolt pierced the very centre of a cross so did not spoil the stone. Another was 'lost'— mortared with other rubble into a rounded pillar at the entrance to a neighbouring house. So little did our grand- fathers care for Christian antiquities! Two bear the chi- rho monogram,[1] in one case with the Greek letters alpha and omega set above it, recalling Revelation 21.6. This stone bears the inscription,

> Here lie holy and distinguished priests, Ides (or *id est* 'that is'), Viventius, and Mavorius.

Within the graveyard there is one great mound, which looks like the place these stones once marked. Kirkmadrine lies eight miles south of Stranraer.

Across this narrowest part of the Irish Sea lies an Irish graveyard, near Newtownards at the north end of Strang- ford Lough. It marks, still consecrated land, the site of the ancient monastery of Moville. I saw no trace of ancient buildings; such may await the excavator. Here was the famous monastic school founded by St Finnian. The train- ing given was doubtless such as Finnian had in his own youth received, and some have claimed that he received it at *Candida Casa*. To this monastic school at Moville there came the young Columba, in the words of his biographer, 'to learn the wisdom of the Scriptures'. If anything from Ninian's Whithorn reached him there, he was to bring it back—and more—when in 563 he crossed the Irish Sea to become Apostle of Scotland.

[1] *XP*, Greek letters for Ch R, 'Christ'.

For St Ninian our sources are limited and late, Bede's eighth-century paragraph and the few additions in Ailred's twelfth-century *Life*. St Patrick is the first Christian in Britain for whom we have direct source material. Trinity College, Dublin, has, as one of its greatest treasures (second only to that wonder of beauty among illuminated manuscripts, the *Book of Kells*), the *Book of Armagh*, and this is itself historically still more wonderful. Most precious of its contents are three lives of St Patrick, numbers 1, 3, and 4 on the list of Patrick material below.

1. *The Confession* This is an autobiography, written, not like St Augustine's in penitence, but in thankful remembrance of God's goodness. The manuscript is over a thousand years old, and ends with this note, 'Thus far the roll which Patrick wrote with his own hand.' The copyist believed that he was looking at the Saint's own writing.

2. *The Letter to Coroticus* This, not in the *Book of Armagh*, we put second because it too claims to be by St Patrick. He writes as Bishop from Ireland to rebuke the soldiers of the King of Strathclyde, whose capital was Dumbarton, for raiding Ireland and killing and enslaving fellow Christians.

3. *Tirechan's Memoir* This describes itself as records 'by word of mouth and in writing from Bishop Ultan', who died in 657.

4. *Muirchu's Life of Patrick* This begins with a dedication to Bishop Aed, who died in 699.

The *Confession* and *Letter to Coroticus* must be Patrick's own. They are simple and artless, written in poor Latin, such as no one would wish to foist upon a bishop and a saint. Their references are, for the time of writing, about 450, exactly right. They call the Franks 'heathen', and so they were till 496. They speak of 'apostate' Picts, as if knowing St Ninian's work a generation earlier. The name Coroticus represents the Ceretic who did, from 420 to 450, rule Strathclyde. More impressive, because harder to get right, among the many Bible quotations, those from the Old Testament are from the Old Latin, while the New Testament ones show the influence of Jerome's revision—just as it should be, since Jerome's New Testament was circulating from 386, while his Old Testament was not completed till 404. All this would demand a discerning and painstaking forger.

With Tirechan and Muirchu we move from the fifth to the seventh century, and opinions differ as to the value of these secondary sources. It seems best in outlining Patrick's course till he sailed as missionary to Ireland, to indicate by 'Patrick says . . .' and 'Tirechan' or 'Muirchu says . . .' the degree of trustworthiness of each part of the story.[1] Dates are uncertain, but for convenience I follow the reckoning of his birth as 389.

Patrick says that at the age of sixteen he was carried from Britain to Ireland, with two sisters, servants, and neighbours, the total prisoners of war being 'many thousands'. In spite of being son and grandson of clergy, religion had meant little to him, but as slave of heathen masters, his prayers became real indeed.

> Day by day as I went, a shepherd with my flock, I used to pray constantly . . . a hundred prayers a day, and nearly as many at night, staying out in the woods or on the mountain. And before daybreak I was up for prayer, in snow or frost or rain.[2]

After six years, a voice in his sleep spoke of home-coming, and a few nights after, 'Your ship is ready.' He escaped, tramped two hundred miles to a port. A ship was ready to sail, and he tried to get a passage but was repulsed. Desperate, and praying hard, he heard a sailor calling him aboard. After three days they landed on a desolate shore (either desolate by nature, or made so by barbarian invasion). Patrick's prayers saved them from starving; they met a herd of pigs.

[1] *Studia Hibernica* 2, 1962. D. A. Binchy, 'Patrick and his Biographers', gives a full review of the many critical problems.
[2] *Confession*, 16.

Well refreshed, even the dogs of the sailors (*eorum*) were full, for many of the latter were worn out and 'left half dead' beside the way (Luke 10.30).[1]

Most translators have imagined dogs littering the path, and accepted Bury's unlikely suggestion that the cargo was Irish wolf-hounds. But why more dogs than two? 'Many of the latter' means 'sailors'. Dogs are mentioned to emphasize their new plenty. It is men half-dead who remind Patrick of the Good Samaritan.

Patrick says that 'after two months' he got away from his shipmates, and then 'after a few years' he got back to Britain. Where did he go meanwhile? Tirechan says that he wandered for seven years

and then spent thirty years, as Bishop Ultan told me, in the island of Lérins.[2]

The Côte d'Azure has different associations for us. The monastery at Lérins, an island off that coast, was founded in 410, a year which called many to flee from a falling world. So Patrick may have been among its earliest visitors. Lupus, later Bishop of Troyes, and colleague of Germanus in Britain in 429 (p. 23), was a monk there then.

Patrick says,

Then after a few years I was in Britain again with my parents, who received me as a son, and besought me, after all I had been through, not to leave them to go anywhere at all.[3]

But he was not to remain in peace.

'I saw in the night visions' (Dan. 7.13), a man coming as if from Ireland, whose name was Victoricus, with letters innumerable. And I read the letter which began, 'The voice of the Irish'. And while I was reading out that beginning, that same moment I thought I heard the voice of those who were beside the wood of Foclut, which is near to the western sea.

[1] *Confession*, 19.
[2] Compare Muirchu's 'thirty years' for his stay at Auxerre. For Lérins three would be more likely. Some critics discount the Lérins, some the whole Gallican tradition.
[3] *Confession*, 23.

And they cried as with one mouth, 'We ask you, holy boy, to come and walk among us once again'. And I was exceedingly 'broken in heart' (Ps. 109.16) and could read no more. And so I awoke. Thanks be to God that after many years the Lord granted to them according to their cry.

Another night, whether in me or beside me, 'I know not; God knoweth' (II Cor. 12.2), in most expert speech which I heard and could not understand, except at the end where it came to this: 'He who laid down his life (John 10.11) for you, it is he who speaks to you.' And so I awoke, rejoicing.

To fulfil his calling he needed training. Patrick mentions this need over and over again, but does not say where he went. Muirchu says that he began to journey to Rome, but found what he needed with

a most holy Bishop, Germanus, at Auxerre, with whom he stayed no little time, some say forty years, some thirty.

Both figures are out of the question.

He may have been ordained as deacon soon after arrival. Muirchu says he was already a presbyter when Germanus sent him with one companion to Ireland. In 429, as we have seen (p. 23), Germanus was invited on a mission of help to Britain. How interested Patrick must have been! The Pope was interested too, and sent to commission Germanus for the task. His messenger was one Palladius, a deacon in Rome who may have belonged to Britain. Germanus, while in Britain, may have heard of Christians among the Irish, and the need for a bishop there. Patrick was waiting for just such a chance, but Patrick was passed over. Palladius was consecrated and sent.

Patrick himself says,

Many were for stopping this mission, saying behind my back, Why should such a one put himself in peril among enemies who know not God? Not out of malice this, but because they thought it unwise, through my being uneducated.[1]

He says that a later attack upon his fitness took place in

[1] *Confession*, 46.

Britain, when he himself was not there, but his 'dearest friend' took his part. Was it Bishop Germanus, at that stage thinking of sending Patrick to Ireland? He says a third attack came from his 'elders' [in the monastery at Auxerre?], and this time they won over

> my dearest friend . . . a man to whom I had entrusted my very soul . . . even him who with his own mouth had told me, You are to be given the rank of Bishop.[1]

This sounds most like Germanus, and Patrick's words, 'I was rejected',[2] sound like dismay at the choice of Palladius. Where was Patrick by this time, already gone to Ireland as presbyter, or still waiting his chance at Auxerre? We cannot be sure. But Muirchu tells us that Palladius was not successful, that he returned from Ireland as far as Britain, and died there. And then at last—432 is taken as the year—Patrick was consecrated in Auxerre, sailed for Britain, journeyed through Britain with the minimum of luggage and the maximum of speed, and so 'with a fair wind he crossed the Irish Sea'.

The *Confession* and *Letter* show two of Patrick's characteristics. First is his sense of never having made good those wasted years from sixteen to twenty-two. He calls himself

> most boorish, least of all the faithful, and contemptible to most.[3]

He says that he has hesitated to write because,

> I am not like those who have studied the law as well as Holy Scripture, and who from infancy have never had to change their speech. . . . Now that I am old, I long for that which when I was young I never acquired.[4]

What then did he get from his years of preparation? The answer is his second characteristic, knowledge of the Bible. In the Latin text which I have used, the *Confession* fills

---

[1] *Confession*, 32. [2] *Confession*, 29.
[3] *Confession*, 1. [4] *Confession*, 9.

21 pages, and the *Letter* 6. The pages average 28 lines. And in these 27 pages are 189 Bible quotations, 7 to a page, one on every fourth line. It was usual for a monk to memorize the Psalter. Patrick quotes more widely, from the Epistles 79 times, Gospels 29, Acts 21, Psalms 21, Prophets 17, and 22 other passages. He must have known great stretches of the Bible by heart.

He is so much a man of one book that he also writes in biblical language. Sometimes this causes misunderstanding, sending critics to emend the text, and historians to go off into elaborate, and irrelevant, explanations. For example, Mr John Godfrey, in *The Church in Anglo-Saxon England*, writes,

> Patrick himself informs us that when he was carried off, he was an unbeliever.[1]

He produces evidence of a surviving heathen temple which may have influenced him. This is beside the point. Patrick says, 'I knew not the true God'.[2] He means that God had not yet spoken to him, as in I Samuel 3.7, 'Samuel did not yet know the Lord'.[3]

Again, Patrick says of his reserve towards his heathen shipmates, when he escaped from Ireland,

> I refused to suck their breasts (*sugere mammellas*) because of the fear of God.[4]

Professor Bury in his *Life of St Patrick*[5] turns to folk-lore, and finds that among some primitive peoples a 'mock birth' has been used in adoption ceremonies. This is ridiculous. Patrick means to say,

> I refused to be too much beholden to them, to redeem my fortunes at their expense, since they were heathen.

While he is wondering how to say it, Isaiah 60.16 comes into his mind,

---

[1] P. 21.   [2] *Confession*, 1.
[3] His later word, 'I did not believe', also refers to lack of saving faith, *Confession*, 27.   [4] *Confession*, 18.   [5] P. 293.

Whereas thou hast been forsaken and hated . . . [and so he had been] . . . thou shalt suck the breast of kings (*suges lac gentium, et mamilla regum lactabris*).[1]

A principle of criticism is not to suggest an elaborate explanation when a simple one will do, especially when the writer is, like Patrick, a simple man.

More important is the last illustration because it concerns a spiritual experience, Patrick's nightmare of assaults by the devil. He asks,

Whence came it to me, into my ignorant mind, to call upon Helias (*Heliam vocarem*)? And at this I saw in the sky the sun rising, and while I was calling Helias with all my might, lo, the splendour of that sun fell upon me.[2]

N. J. D. White, in *St Patrick, his Writings and Life*, turns to the Greek *helios* (sun) for explanation, and mentions the prevalence of sun-worship in the late Roman Empire. The point surely is, not that Patrick, when he recounted this experience, knew the Greek word *helios*, but that he knew Matthew 27.45ff.

. . . darkness until the ninth hour. And about the ninth hour, Jesus cried with a loud voice. . . . And some said, This man calleth Elijah (*Heliam vocat*).

Patrick says that the sun rose, because in the Gospel, after our Lord's last cry, the darkness was over. He goes on to say that he believes it was the Spirit of Christ who thus called out for his sake, and trusts that it will be so in his day of trouble. Yes, Patrick knew his Bible.

One mystery remains. Where was Patrick's home? Three passages are important:

My father was Calpurnius, a deacon, one of the sons of Potitus, a presbyter, who belonged to the village of Banavemtaberniae. He had a farm close by, where I was taken captive.[3]

[1] Thus in Vulgate; the Old Latin would be similar.
[2] *Confession*, 20.   [3] *Confession*, 1.

To the soldiers of Coroticus. Because of their evil deeds, I will say not 'my fellow citizens', nor 'citizens with the holy Romans' but 'citizens with demons' rather.[1]

Should I ever have come to Ireland, apart from God, or according to the flesh? Who was there to constrain me? It is because 'I am bound in the spirit' (Acts 20. 22) that I have left the sight of all my kindred. Do you think that of myself I should show a godly pity towards that people which once took me captive and destroyed the menservants and maidservants of my father's house? I was born a freeman according to the flesh, with a decurion for my father. But I have sold my nobility, without a blush or a second thought, in the service of others; and so in Christ I am slave to a foreign nation, for the sake of the unspeakable glory of 'eternal life, which is in Christ Jesus our Lord' (Rom. 6.23). And if my own know me not, 'a prophet hath no honour in his own country' (John 4.44).[2]

First, Banavemtaberniae has little to tell us. We do not even know how to carve it up into separate words. Circumstances seem to demand a place, to borrow words from Muirchu, 'not far from our [Irish] sea'. This rules out the promising Roman place-name Banaventa, almost as far inland as possible, near Daventry. Three estuaries seem to be most likely, the Clyde, the Severn, and the Solway.

On the Clyde lay the capital of Coroticus (Ceretic)'s Kingdom of Strathclyde. Throughout the Middle Ages it was assumed that Patrick's words, 'my fellow-citizens . . . my own (people) . . . own country . . .' meant that he belonged to that kingdom. Eighth- and tenth-century notes say, 'His origin was of the Britons of Strathclyde', and name his birth-place as Ail-Cluade (Rock of the Clyde), i.e. the rock which gives Dum-Barton its name, 'Fortress of the Britons'. Two miles upstream from there lies Old Kilpatrick. Patrick's words are often taken as being of wider reference, that he too is a Briton, or a Roman, but this interpretation is something quite new.

One factor in turning eyes southwards was the recogni-

---

[1] *Letter to Coroticus*, 2.   [2] *Letter*, 10. 11.

tion of a second Ceretic, the Welshman who, a generation after his namesake of Strathclyde, gave his name to Cardiganshire. Following this clue, someone reported no less than three Banwens in Glamorganshire.[1] The Welsh king is sometimes favoured because of date, but many have turned back to the northern Ceretic—without remembering to turn back to a northern Patrick.

On the Solway, a Roman place-name Banna is thought to have belonged to the western end of Hadrian's Wall.[2] Some prefer the Solway to the Clyde because of the degree of continued Romanization implied by Patrick's 'decurion' father. *Decurio* meant 'town-councillor', but by this time it belonged, like much else, to a debased currency. The municipality included wide country areas around, and the *curia* was composed, not so much of elected councillors, as of members of a class, now hereditary, owning a certain amount of land, and required to take responsibility for the finance of local government and public works, and for the community's share of imperial taxation. In most of the empire people born into this class had long been trying to escape the decurion's burdens. It may be a sign of Patrick's living beyond effective Roman administration that he should boast of his inheritance of such 'nobility'.[3]

I confess that, living on the Firth of Clyde, and able to look eastward up river to Dumbarton's famous Rock, and south-west between the mountains to the entrance to the Irish Sea, I have a certain prejudice. But do not ask me to lay it aside until you can show me a more likely place for the Briton who became Apostle of Ireland.

In the *Confession* Patrick summarizes the achievements of his mission.

How is it that in Ireland, where they never had the knowledge of God, but only worshipped idols and abominations, always until now, there has lately come to be 'a people prepared for

[1] Bury, *Life of Patrick*, x and 322-5.
[2] The Brampton site, see p. 33, footnote 2.
[3] Samuel Dill, *Roman Society in the Last Century of the Western Empire*, pp. 250-2.

the Lord' (Luke 1.17), and they are called children of God?
Sons of the Scots, and daughters of their rulers are seen as
monks and virgins of Christ.[1]

And at the very end he adds,

I beseech those who believe in God and fear him, whoever
deigns to look at or receive this writing, which Patrick the
sinner, yes, the unlearned, wrote in Ireland, say not that it
was ignorant I, who had anything to do or to show for God's
good pleasure. You shall thus judge and hold as very truth—
it was the gift of God. And this is my confession before I die.[2]

The year of Patrick's death, 461, is also the year of Pope
Leo's. And here are Pope Leo's words beginning to be
fulfilled by Patrick's work of Christian expansion in the
far north-west:

What your [Rome's] toils in war subdued is less than what the
peace of Christ has conquered.

One century more, and from Ireland the Church would
cross to claim North Britain, and reach much farther north
than ever in Rome's imperial day.

Before following further this unexpected Christian
expansion in the far north-west, we need to look again at
the Western Roman Empire's continued decline. If the
early part of the fifth century was, for men of discernment
like Jerome and Augustine, full of the sound of doom,
could anyone miss the omens when that century's last
quarter was reached? The irony of fate produced as the
last Western Emperor a youth with the two names Romulus
Augustus, as if to recall the founders of the City and of the
Empire, now when the end of both seemed near. History
with justice prefers to remember him by the derisive dimin-
utive, Augustulus. It was the end, however men tried to
disguise change with pretence. In some lands, invaders
respected Roman forms, themselves adopted some of them,
and liked to feel a veneer of civilization giving respectability
to their new kingdoms. In others, barbarian soldiery left

---

[1] *Confession*, 41.   [2] *Confession*, 62.

to the despoiled 'Roman' population its civil officials, courts, and laws, in a parallel, almost extra-territorial, existence.

In Italy itself Augustus was deposed in 476 by Odovacar, who commanded the German mercenaries. Odovacar preferred that his own rule should be untrammelled by pretence, so the Senate obligingly sent the imperial insignia to Constantinople, saying that they no longer needed their own Emperor, and asking that Odovacar be given the title of Patrician. In 490 Theodoric, King of the Ostrogoths, ousted Odovacar and stepped into his place. In this he acted as agent of the Emperor Zeno. His life continued in this dual role, a Gothic King, who repaired Roman aqueducts and public buildings, and gave to harassed Italy thirty-six years of peace.

Gaul, south of the Loire and west of the Rhône, was already recognized as part of the Visigothic kingdom which extended over most of Spain. Here not even a nominal acknowledgement of the Roman Empire survived. These Goths took two-thirds of the land—one-third being the customary price of what was pleasantly called 'hospitality' —and cared only for their own Empire as Rome's successor.

In 477 the Vandal Gaiseric died, founder of a kingdom in North Africa and a sea-power which ruled the Mediterranean. The Vandals were anti-Roman, and lived in absolute separation from the conquered, who might pretend, if they wished, that their own Roman ways continued.

In northern Gaul, the Franks, long settled on both banks of the Rhine, were extending their power westward. In 481 Clovis, a boy of sixteen, became their king. Four years later he defeated a Roman army, chose Paris as his capital, and effectively replaced the province of Gaul by the kingdom of the Franks. He came into territories with large areas depopulated, so had no need to antagonize landowners to reward new Frankish settlers. He incorporated defeated Roman mercenaries into his own armies. Secure in the goodwill of northern Gaul, he pressed upon the Visigoths beyond the Loire, protected Gaul against the Allemani from the Upper Rhine, and in 493 married the daughter of the King of the Burgundians, thus securing a useful ally to the south. The future of Europe lay with these virile Franks, and their society marks the emergence, from the ruin of the old Roman economy—centralized, city-based, dependent upon wide communications—of a simpler feudal society, based on ownership of local land.

The years 449 to 455 are marked by Bede as the real beginning of the invasion of Britain. The waterways most inviting first to the pirates, then to the settlers, were the Solent, the Thames estuary, the Wash, and the Humber. Bede assigns the Jutes to Kent, the Isle of Wight and its surroundings; the Saxons to Essex, Sussex and Wessex, as these names imply: and the Angles to the Midlands and the north, a preponderance explaining why the whole would soon be Angle-land. The Anglo-Saxons cared little for what had preceded them. Even in place-names, not many Latin or British words remain. Of the inhabitants, many perished, many more fled to the west country or the Continent, and those who remained were not such as to contribute to the civilizing of their conquerors. The break with the Roman past was almost complete.

The Western Roman Empire which was thus passing away was the Christian Roman Empire, so we must ask, What of the Christian religion in all this change?

The peoples of Germanic stock had most of them been touched by Christianity of a sort, either before or soon after they moved into Roman territory. In almost every case it was not the Christianity of the Imperial State Church, of the first four Councils (Nicea 325, Constantinople 381, Ephesus 431, Chalcedon 451), and of the historic Creeds which the Fathers meeting there had framed. It was Arian Christianity. And Arius had not ascribed to Jesus Christ full divinity (nor, for that matter, real humanity), but had thought of him more nearly as the heathen thought of a demi-god. But if these Germans did not have so adequate a theological expression for their Christian faith, they did, as early as the year 341, have Bishop Ulfilas, who saw that the Bible and Liturgy in Latin would not do, and that he must labour to put both into Gothic language. Arian Christianity spread from tribe to tribe, not so much because Arians had compromised with heathen thought, but because their faith was expressed in German language,— in a word, not because they were bad theologians, but because they were good missionaries. The saving factor in this fifth century of loss was the survival of the Christian religion. But while a common faith might have been ex- pected to unite the invaders and the older elements in the population, enmity between Arians and Catholics became one further cause of division, and, in North Africa and Spain, of persecution.

To all this there were two exceptions, the Franks and the Anglo-Saxons. They were not Christians of any kind, but heathen. Yet Clovis was careful to show respect for the Church, its bishops, and its property. And the Burgundian princess whom he married, in the providence of God, was a Christian, not Arian but Catholic. This was to be a factor of great importance, as we shall see. Across the Channel, Britain was fast becoming paganized, and in this case there was—or so it seemed—no saving factor. And then in the year 496 came two events which secured for western Europe a Christian future, intimately connected, both of them, with the Christian religion's re-entry into England.

First, in the year 496 Clovis, King of the Franks, with three thousand of his warriors, was baptized on Christmas Day. Gregory, Bishop of Tours (540-594), says in the pro- logue to his *History of the Franks* that he wrote it for the sake of those who 'were in despair because the end of the world drew near'. He begins the story of Clovis's conversion by telling of the Christian witness of Clotilda, trying to prove to her husband that his heathen gods were false. It shakes one's confidence in this historian to observe that the names of the gods which he puts into her mouth are those of classical antiquity. The Bishop of Tours was not of Frankish but of Roman descent. But we must not assume that he was unintelligent enough to recite by mistake 'Mars, Jupiter, Mercury', and the rest. A non-literary religion does speedily fade once its altars are overthrown and its priests dispersed. It may well be that, one century after, the Bishop had never heard the names of the gods of the Franks. Perhaps, without knowing the details, we may accept it as likely that the influence, so often decisive in a man's life, and not least with regard to religion, was decisive here—his wife's. The decision, however, did fit Clovis's policy of unifying Gallo-Roman and Frankish peoples, and of extending his territory by standing for great causes. He could now drive the Visigoths out of south Gaul because 'the presence of Arianism grieved him'. He could finally defeat the Alemanni, and so begin an expansion east of the Rhine which was big with promise. His successors for centuries would be patrons of the conversion of all the German lands.

Gregory of Tours is more convincing when he quotes Clovis, not yet baptized, making this prayer before battle with the Alemanni. Even in the Bishop's Latin it sounds short, sharp, and business-like:

> I have called upon my own gods, but, as I see it, they are far from my help. I believe they are robbed of power, who do not help those who give them obedience. I now call upon thee, and believe in thee. So let me be plucked from the hands of my adversaries.

It worked, and so he was baptized, and then went on to rout them utterly. True too to the spirit of the times is Gregory's description of the baptism in the great church at Reims:

> The aisles were hung with embroidered awnings. The baptistry was prepared, with balsams sprinkled. Candles blazed and

gleamed, and the whole sanctuary was filled with a divine
fragrance, as it were the fragrance of Paradise itself.

And as King Clovis knelt in the font, waiting for the water
to be poured over him, Archbishop Remi thundered forth,

> Bow low your neck!
> Burn what you have worshipped!
> Worship what before you burned!

It seems at least a promising beginning that later, hearing
the Archbishop expound the Jews' rejection of their Lord
for the Romans to crucify, King Clovis should have exclaimed, 'If only I and my faithful Franks had been there!'

The religious content of this conversion may be doubted.
Of its results for the Christian religion there can hardly be
room for doubt. Milman calls it 'the most important event,
in its remote as well as its immediate consequences, in
European history'[1]. Latourette, on the other hand, says, 'Its
importance can be exaggerated . . . If Clovis had not become a Christian, his successors would . . . . If he had been
an Arian, the west would not have abandoned its ortho-
doxy.'[2] Yet, as a matter of fact, this was the way. The
example of the triumphant Franks speeded the turning of
the other new nations from Arianism to the Catholic faith.

As for the connection with England, the great-grand-
daughter of Clotilda followed the example of her ancestress.
She was given in marriage to the heathen King of Kent.
In 597, one hundred and one years from the baptism of
Clovis, it was she who opened England's door to the mission-
aries.

The second event must belong to about the same year,
496, for the man concerned was born in 480 and it happened
when he was in his 'teens. He was sent to complete his
education in Rome. It was later said, 'He inspected the
world and despised it.' Disgusted with the immorality of

---

[1] *History of Latin Christianity*, I, 349.
[2] *Expansion of Christianity*, I, 208.

the decadent city, he went off to live as a hermit in a cave. This may seem too trivial to notice, when a civilization was passing, and new nations were coming to birth. This youth came from Nursia, eighty miles north-east of Rome; he died at Monte Cassino, about eighty miles south-east of Rome, with the cave, Subiaco, almost half way between. And we do not hear of his going anywhere else at all. So it was no impressive inspection of the world, and in any case he decided not to face it. Yet, judging events by their power to change the world, we must place Benedict's renunciation before the conversion of a king.

In every age the spread of Christianity has been the work, not of the generality of Christians, but of the more devoted few. In the Church of the first three centuries such devotion might mean prison and death. And these the Church honoured as witnesses beyond all others, keeping for them the special names of confessors and martyrs.

Monasticism began when the Church's struggle with the Roman world was over,[1] and the movement proceeded apace, when, under the pro-Christian Constantine, 312 onwards, 'the peace of Christ' had come. It was a time of temptation to worldliness, and the easy acceptance of a nominal Christianity. The monk stood in protest against such a decline. If the world had accepted our religion, he insisted that our religion must still deny the world. Persecution had ceased. Martyrdom was no longer the price of devotion. But being a Christian could never be easy, and he must see that it was not. This is, of course, only one aspect of monasticism, but it is an aspect which recognizes the monk as now representing that devoted minority, upon which Christian expansion still depends. The monk is the medieval missionary.

The importance of St Benedict is that his contribution becomes determinative of monasticism in all the west, and it is a typical Roman contribution. The abuses besetting

---

[1] Or rather, in a generation of peace, 260-303, when it seemed to be over.

this movement were idleness, ignorance, vagrancy, fanaticism. Benedict contributed discipline. His *Rule*, given in the year 529, begins,

> Give heed, my son, to the precepts of the master, and incline the ear of your heart. Accept with gladness the admonition of the father, and fulfil it carefully. So by the hard work (*labor*) of obedience, you may return, whence the sloth (*desidia*, 'sitting-down') of disobedience has withdrawn you.

The more devoted minority was now to be found among the monks. In those of Benedict's Order that minority was not only devoted but disciplined, just the men the Church would need for a mission to the far north-west.

It is appropriate that the oldest manuscript of the Rule of St Benedict should lie in the Bodleian at Oxford. The first Benedictine house to be established beyond the limits of St Benedict's own Italy was the mission-station of Augustine at Canterbury, in the year 597.

III

The Northern Celtic Mission

ST COLUMBA is for all Great Britain a figure of importance beyond any we have mentioned yet, as Apostle of Scotland, and as founder of that Celtic mission which, from St Aidan (635) onwards, was to be the agent for converting the greater part of England too. He is also the first Celtic Christian, apart from St Patrick, whom we are able really to know as a person. The source of our knowledge is the *Life of St Columba* written by Adamnan, Abbot of Iona from 679 to 704.

He wrote about ninety-three years after Columba's death, too late for him to have direct contact with those who knew the saint. He claims to tell of

> things handed down in the consistent records of our elders, and of faithful experienced men, . . . committed to writing . . . or learned by hearing.

Of records in writing one was *The Miracles of St Columba*, written by Cummene, also Abbot of Iona, who died ten years before Adamnan's appointment. Even he could not have known many eye-witnesses. Bede says, 'Some writings are said to have come down from his disciples.' Adamnan names some sources, in such words as these: '. . . as he himself bore witness in the presence of those from whom we have learned these things.' '. . . This man's sister's son gave me the account.' Sometimes, reading Adamnan, one suspects that there may have been a body of material, either oral or written, connected with one person, who recurs, central in a series of incidents, e.g. Baithene, Columba's kinsman and successor, and Diormit, his attendant.

In a brief introduction, Adamnan tells us that Columba is the Latin equivalent of the Hebrew 'Jonah', meaning 'dove', a good name for the simple man in whom the Holy Spirit made his dwelling. The coming of a such a one had been foretold by Mochta, a Briton, disciple of Patrick. Columba's father was Fergus, his mother Ethne, both 'of noble blood'. Adamnan might have put 'royal' instead of 'noble'. Fergus, we know, was great-grandson of Niall, High-King of Ireland when Patrick was taken as slave. Adamnan ends his introduction with this notable passage:

> In the second year after the battle of Cul-drebene [i.e. 563], when he was forty-two, he wished to go on pilgrimage (*peregrinari*) for the sake of Christ, and sailed from Ireland to Britain. From boyhood he had given himself as a Christian recruit to studies in quest of wisdom. God bestowed on him a sound body and a pure mind, and these he so guarded as to show that, even while here on earth, he was fitted for the life of heaven. For he was angelic in appearance, bright in speech, holy in deeds, excellent in gifts, and great in counsel. For thirty-four years he served as soldier in an island garrison. He could not let an hour go by without applying himself to prayer, reading, writing, or some sort of work. Day and night without ceasing he was engaged with an unwearied round of fasts and vigils, the burden of any part of which might have seemed more than a man could bear. And in it all he was dear to everybody, always showed a cheerful holy face, and in his inmost heart was made glad with the joy of the Holy Spirit.

Being given such a preview, one is eager to go on to the *Life*. Adamnan's work has the limitations characteristic of medieval hagiography. The author sets out, not to follow the stages of a man's life, but to persuade us that this man was a saint. Adamnan announces that Book I will be about his prophetic gifts, Book II about his miraculous powers, and Book III about visions of angels. Many things which we most want to know Adamnan does not tell us, and much that he does tell we hesitate to accept as fact. But do not put the book impatiently aside. One must come to this subject prepared to dig for history underneath the marvels. Can we expect much history there?

The latest critical edition,[1] *Adomnan's Life of Columba* (1961), says,

> Apart from what can be inferred from Adomnan's account, very little is known of Columba. The Middle-Irish Life, a homily, supplies nothing . . . historical.

This judgement I accept. The authors continue,

> Adomnan had too little genuine tradition . . . to write a Life. . . . His value is less for history of Columba than for his own ideas and for the circumstances of his own times.

So Columba fades away into the shadows, with the majority of the Celtic saints.

Now this does not make sense. In 1928 vivid memories of David Livingstone were found among illiterate Africans in a place through which he had passed sixty years before.[2] The time between Columba's death (597) and Adamnan's writing (690) is half as long again. But the monks of Iona were not illiterate, and the great man was not just passing through, but living there for thirty-four years. Who can doubt that strange experiences and striking sayings were written down, that a man would pass a story to his sister's son, that these things remained, vivid still, when Cummene and Adamnan took up their pens to write?

This point of view, that the Columba stories communicate Adamnan's ideas and seventh-century customs rather than Columba's history, leads the authors to what seem to me forced, and therefore false, interpretations. For example, the death of Brito (p. 57) I read as a recollection of the first death among the Iona monks, when Columba, after giving his blessing, 'hurried out because he could not bear to see him die' (*nolens videre morientem*). The Andersons' Introduction marks this as written to remind 'the abbot that, as

---

[1] A. O. and M. O. Anderson.
[2] C. P. Groves, *Planting of Christianity in Africa*, II, 335.

a priest, he must not be polluted by presence at a death', and a footnote in the text adds, 'Reconsecration [*sic*; only a bishop is consecrated] would have been needed to remove the pollution.' This is misleading. Some Irish priests seem to have been influenced by Leviticus 21. So far from giving us reason to include Columba among them, Adamnan mentions four cases where Columba was present at a death.[1] Again, when, with his own death approaching, Columba tells Diormit that it is Saturday, the Sabbath, the Andersons introduce three pages about the Sabbatical controversy in Adamnan's time, i.e. regarding the transference of Sabbath observance to the Lord's Day. All that Columba means is what he says, 'For me, truly Sabbath, since today is the last of my laborious life' (p. 69).

Many historians of Columba have been uncritical about their sources, but here is criticism which misses the obvious point of a story.

At the end of his book Adamnan says,

> This same man of blessed memory has received this special grace, that in spite of living in our remote little island of Britain, his fame has reached as far as the peninsula of Spain, the Gauls, Italy which lies over the Alps, even to that City of cities, Rome itself.

The justification for the idea of digging underneath Adamnan's stories must be in what we can find. So, let us dig.

Iona is a speck of an island, three miles from north to south, and one and a half miles across at its widest, off the south-west tip of Mull, open to the winds of the Atlantic. We see the monks gathering a boat-load of twigs from a peasant's field, for their wattle buildings, and compensating the not too willing peasant—for in these wind-swept islands trees are few—with the gift of three bushels of quick-growing barley (the growth of which is recorded as miraculous.)[2] They use a fleet of twelve coracles with full

---

[1] I, 33, 45; II, 25, 32; III, 14. For the Christian regard for Levitical uncleanness, cf. reference on p. 79 to Augustine and Leviticus 15.

[2] II, 3.

sail, to tow oak beams for repairing their monastery. This is confessedly in Adamnan's time, but its first construction would surely be similar.[1] Of the monastic buildings, Adamnan mentions *hospitium*, the guest-house, which the monks 'make ready, drawing water to wash the feet of the guests';[2] the wooden church, central in their daily lives, with its regular cycle of worship, and a small side-chapel where one could go for private prayer, with a door between;[3] the huts for the monks, with the Abbot's lodging described in some detail. Of farm buildings he mentions the barn, the byre with a horse to carry milk pails to the monastery, a mill for grinding corn,[4] and a kiln, *canaba*, i.e. a hut with a stove for drying the harvest in this rainy west-land. All was enclosed by *vallum*, an earthen wall.[5] Following just these clues from Adamnan, Dr Charles Thomas,[6] between 1956 and 1959, did actual excavations. He traced the whole course of the *vallum*, 1,100 by 500 feet, fixed one mound as the site of the barn, and stones in a hollow as the kiln. He found that Columba's hut stood 100 feet west of the present abbey, just as Adamnan says, 'on high ground'.[7] It is a ridge widened to hold the hut by an embankment of boulders on either side, so *in tabulis*[8] means, not 'on planks' or 'with a wooden floor', as hitherto translated, but 'on a platform'. A flat slab of rock recalls the words, 'for mattress the bare rock, and a stone for a pillow'.[9]

Adamnan shows us the monks fishing and farming like their island neighbours. Columba sends two over to Mull to intercept a robber who is hiding his boat among the sandhills, so that at nightfall he can cross to a rock where seals breed, the property of the monastery, to kill and steal their young.

We see them at work as farmers. Adamnan thinks it not irrelevant to record a spiritual comfort which Columba's

---

[1] II, 46.   [2] I, 4.   [3] III, 19.   [4] III, 23.   [5] II, 39.
[6] Of the Department of Archaeology, University of Edinburgh, to whom I am grateful for much help and information.
[7] III, 22.   [8] I, 25.   [9] III, 23.

monks once felt. Returning in the evening after harvesting they came to a place half way between Iona's western plain and the monastery. Here each one seemed to feel something wonderful and strange, but no one ventured to remark upon it to the others, till Baithene, who was then managing the work . . . bade them speak out. 'For days past', said one of the seniors, 'I have felt some fragrance, as if all flowers were gathered into one; a feeling of warmth, not burning but comfortable; a strange joy in my heart which makes me forget sadness and toil. Yes, and though the load I carry on my back is heavy, from here to the monastery it grows light, how I know not, but I am burdened no longer.' . . . Baithene replied, 'It is our old master, Columba, mindful of our toil, and anxious because we are so late home. And, since he cannot come to meet us in the body, he sends his spirit to refresh and rejoice us.'[1]

We see the care with which some followed their more distinctive craft as copyists. Columba himself is said to have been skilled at this. Adamnan several times mentions his copying a manuscript (as on p. 70), and also gives us this little picture. Baithene asks Columba to allow one of the brethren to look over the Psalter which he has copied, as we might read proof for one another. Columba may have replied jocularly, 'Why waste his time? I'd be surprised if he found more than a single stroke missing.' One letter 'i' was omitted, and this is recounted as one example of the Saint's prophetic gift.[2]

Among the brethren we hear of two who are *Saxo* (which stands for English, as does the Gaelic 'Sassenach'[3]), one of them a baker.[4] Another foreigner was *Brito*, a Briton. Adamnan tells the tender little story of his death. When he was suddenly taken ill, Columba went to give him his blessing, but then stepped outside, for he 'could not bear to see him die'. And there outside, another monk found him 'lost in wonder', so that he knelt before the Saint and asked what he had seen.

[1] I, 29. [2] I, 23.
[3] In spite of Scotland's nearest neighbours being the Angles of Northumbria. [4] III,10. 22.

'I saw angels warring with the powers of evil, and the angels have prevailed, and carried to the joy of the heavenly home this pilgrim, the first of us to die upon this island.'[1]

We get glimpses of that which was most distinctive of the monastic life, the cycle of worship in the church, where they came every three hours through the day, and again, 'the bell tolls in the middle of the night,'[2] and on Sundays and Feast Days for the Eucharist.[3] Apart from the regular hours, there were times when Columba's handbell would summon them, even 'at dead of night',[4] when by holy intuition he knew that someone was in dire need of their prayers. Here is one example. Cormac, one of Columba's monks at Durrow in Ireland, was seeking an island solitude in the far north, and his coracle was in danger.

> Our holy Columba, though distant in body, in spirit was with him in the boat, and that very moment rang his bell, calling the brethren to prayer. He entered the church and addressed those standing around, 'Brothers, earnestly pray for Cormac and his sailors, blown north by the wind for fourteen days, that God will turn it, and bring back this craft out of danger.' And he knelt before the altar and prayed to almighty God, who rules the wind and all things. Then he rises quickly and says, 'Now, Brothers, let us rejoice with those for whom we prayed. For the Lord will change the wind and bring our comrades back.'[5]

Adventurous journeys were mostly over the sea. That was the element to cross wherever they went from their island base. And they founded branch monasteries—mission stations, we might call them—some in other islands, on Tiree and on Hinba (probably Colonsay or Jura), and one on Loch Awe,[6] and there was much coming and going between them. More than once we find the Saint praying for his monks' coracles, and once for his own, when

[1] III, 6.   [2] III, 23.   [3] III, 11.   [4] I, 22.   [5] II, 42.
[6] There may well have been others already in the Saint's life-time, but these are mentioned by Adamnan (I, 21, 30, 31).

he stopped bailing out the green water, and began to pour forth fervent prayers.[1]

Once he was comforted in a storm by a vision of a friend in Ireland, St Kenneth, sensing his danger, and rising from table so quickly that he left one shoe behind.

'Ah, Kenneth, your dash to the church with one shoe off is much to our advantage.'[2]

We hear of other dangers:

Loathsome creatures, covering the sea, washed against the ship's bottom, the sides, both stem and stern, about the size of frogs and with terrible stings, swarming over the blades of the oars.[3]

This sounds like a plague of jelly-fish.
Brother Berach, sailing to Tiree, suddenly met

a whale rising like a mountain afloat, mouth wide open, all bristling with teeth.[4]

There were adventures too in journeys by land. In the island of Skye, Columba

went on alone, at a distance from the brethren, to say his prayers, entering into a dense wood, and lo, a boar of extraordinary size . . .[5]

The most horrific of wild beasts encountered, however, was in Inverness. I translate this passage in full, as the earliest reference to the Loch Ness monster.

When the Saint was in the province of the Picts, he had to cross the River Ness. On reaching the bank, he saw villagers burying a poor fellow, who, they said, a little before, had been swimming there. A water-beast with most savage jaws had caught and bitten him. Some of them had put out in a boat, but too late to do more than drag the river to recover the poor corpse.
    The Saint listened to this, and said, 'All the same, one of

[1] II, 12.   [2] II, 13.   [3] II, 42.   [4] I, 19.   [5] II, 26.

our company must swim to the opposite shore and steer the boat there back to me.' When he heard this command of the worthy Saint, Luigni Mocu-min instantly obeyed, stripped to his shirt, and dived into the water.

His former prey had sharpened the monster's appetite rather than assuaged it. He was lying hidden in deep water. But feeling the surface disturbed by the swimmer, up he came with a roar, jaws wide open, making straight for Luigni in midstream.

The Saint saw it, and while the natives and even the brethren were terror-stricken, he just raised his holy hand to save him, drew the sign of the cross in the empty air, and commanded the fierce beast in the name of God, saying, 'No further! Do not touch him! Quick! Back you go!' The beast was so near Luigni that there was but a pole's length between. But at the Saint's call it drew back as quickly as if hauled by cables, and fled away.

The brothers saw the beast go, saw their comrade Luigni back in the boat safe and sound, and with great wonder gave glory to God for the blessed man. And the heathen natives, seeing with their own eyes so great a miracle, were constrained to say, 'Great is the God of the Christians!'[1]

There were dangers too from men. One night when north of the Grampians, among the heathen Picts, they stayed in a lakeside village. Columba roused his companions in the night and sent them, sleepy as they were, to move their coracle which a neighbour had housed for the night. Later he called to Diormit, 'Go out and look at that part of the village where first you put the boat. An enemy has done this.' It was all going up in flames.[2]

The first four sections of Book III, on visions of angels, make important additions to our knowledge of Columba. The first, history or no, is the story of an annunciation. Ethne, during her pregnancy, dreams of an angel who says to her,

'You shall bear a son, who shall be numbered among God's prophets. Countless the souls he shall bring home to heaven.'

[1] II, 27. [2] I, 34.

The second names the priest who brought up Columba, Irish royalty apparently not being content with nannies and tutors but putting out their children to foster-parents. With this 'man of admirable life' may lie the secret of Columba's call to the Church's service. Strangely enough, though Adamnan does not remark upon it, his name, Cruithnechan, means 'little Pict'.

The fourth section mentions 'the venerable Bishop Finnian, his former teacher'. There is a similar reference earlier.

> In his youth he stayed with St Finnian the Bishop, to learn the wisdom of the Scriptures. . . . He was then a deacon.[1]

Thus casually does Adamnan refer to his beginning the monastic life at Moville, which is his link with *Candida Casa* and St Ninian (p. 34). In this fourth section quoted above, Adamnan proceeds,

> It was in those days that the Saint sailed over to Britain with twelve comrades, disciples of his.

One great question is his motive for so doing, and for that we turn back to the third section of Book III, which tells of Columba's being

> excommunicated by a certain synod, not rightly, as in the end was shown.

Later tradition connects this with the battle of Cul-drebene (p. 53). Columba is said to have called for his clansmen's support against the High-King of Ireland because of two grievances. First, Columba had copied a Psalter owned by Finnian, and because it was made without permission Finnian claimed the copy. When asked for judgement, the King said,

> 'To every cow her calf,
> to every book its copy.'

[1] II, 1.

and decided for Finnian. Second, the King had arrested and executed a fugitive to whom Columba, as a priest, had given sanctuary. The clan rose in his support, and in the battle three thousand were slain. This, it is said, was why a Church synod excommunicated him. Other Irish sources enlarge upon Columba's remorse, his acceptance of the penance of leaving Ireland for ever, his decision to win for Christ three thousand souls from among the heathen in recompense. Adamnan knows nothing of this. He mentions the battle, well known in Irish history, as marking the time, not as being the cause, of Columba's departure. He mentions the excommunication without connecting it with the battle, or giving any reason. According to him, so far from leaving Ireland for ever, Columba continued to rule his Irish monasteries, returned several times, and was there held in high honour. As for Columba's motive in coming to Iona, he merely says, 'He wished to go on pilgrimage for the sake of Christ.'

Many have accepted this later tradition, feeling that Adamnan gives it some support by mentioning the battle in connection, even if not in causal connection, with Columba's coming, and by mentioning the excommunication. I find this even harder to swallow than most of Adamnan's marvels. I suggest that the tradition arose because Adamnan's word for Columba's motive seemed inadequate, 'pilgrimage'. Here were a battle and an excommunication. Why not use both to explain Columba's leaving his native land, by making the battle his sin, the excommunication his guilt, and leaving Ireland his punishment? A typical monkish quarrel over a manuscript, and a dispute where disputes often arose between king and priest, this difficult matter of sanctuary—these would be easy and picturesque additions.[1]

[1] Two extremes are represented by W. D. Simpson, *The Historical St Columba* (3rd edition, revised, 1963), and the Andersons' *Adomnan's Life of Columba* (1961). The first accepts the exile and its causes as 'established beyond question', and says, 'Adamnan glosses over the exile very tactfully' (p. 113). The second says, 'The battle of Cul-

As a matter of fact Adamnan's statement of motive is adequate. It is a motive characteristic of the Celtic monk. We have seen that the monk is the medieval missionary (p. 50). Monasticism comes to two modes of missionary expression, the first incidental, the second purposeful. Both are seen, as seldom elsewhere in so clear and striking a contrast, in the conversion of this land of ours. Preparation for the purposeful we have already seen. The Benedictines provided the Church with just such a task force as was needed for some strategic operation (p. 51). We shall soon see Pope Gregory the Great as the strategist who sent Augustine and his Benedictines, less than fifty years after St Benedict's own time. About the mission there was nothing incidental. It was planned in every detail. In Columba we see the other type.

Monks, in their attempt at the more wholly committed life, often felt called to further renunciation. St Antony himself began the ascetic life in his own village; then moved to a ruin by the Nile; then further into the desert; till at the last he had crossed Egypt to within sight of the Red Sea. There is an oft-quoted saying of the Desert Fathers, 'Except a man shall say, I alone, and God, are in this world, he shall not find peace.' We have noticed in the west this monkish quest for alone-ness, at *Candida Casa*, where there is St Ninian's Cave (p. 32), and in Adamnan's account of Cormac's sailing north in his coracle for fourteen days, 'seeking a *desert* in the sea' (p. 58). Where there was no desert, there was the chance of 'pilgrimage', like the call of Abraham,

Get thee out of thy country, and from thy kindred, and from thy father's house.

---

drebene was a turning point in [Irish] history. . . . Little is known of the cause. . . . If this legend [of Columba's guilt] was in existence in Adomnan's time, he deliberately rejected or contradicted it' (p. 73). I reached my own conclusion from the sources independently, or rather from Adamnan, our only real source. I have not changed it in the direction of either. To judge Adamnan's silence as guileful is to prejudge the issue. To call it contradiction is to overstate the case.

Not in this case to go to a promised land, it is to 'seek a
city which hath the foundations, whose maker and builder
is God'. And then, leaving homeland, they find themselves
among the heathen, and being devoted Christians, they do
the Christian thing, incidentally. 'He wished to go on
pilgrimage.' Yes, that is enough, or almost enough. With
Columba there is one fact more. From those willing to join
his pilgrimage he chose twelve, and twelve is a number
which begins to change the pilgrimage into an apostolate,
a mission.

How did they set about their task as missionaries? Bede
describes the mission:

> Columba came to preach the word of God to the provinces
> of the Northern Picts, separated from the Southern Picts
> by the [Grampian] mountains.[1]

Here follows the paragraph already quoted (p. 30) about
the earlier work of Ninian among the Southern Picts.

Adamnan tells of Columba's first journey to King Brude.
Probably it was soon after they settled on Iona, dependent
upon the goodwill of the Pictish King if they were to
remain. As the river Zambesi and Lakes Nyasa and
Tanganyika provided a highway for Livingstone into
darkest Africa, so on a smaller scale—150 miles instead of
1,300—that great cleft through the Highlands, Lochs
Linnhe, Lochy, and Ness, would be his route. Coracles,
light wicker work with a covering of hide, were admirable
for inland waterways, easy to carry where they could not
be sailed. Brude's fortress was where Inverness now stands.
The journey, easy compared with most cross-country
journeys then, was not without its dangers, for the Picts had
recently attacked and defeated the immigrant Scots of
Dalriada. Adamnan, intent as ever on the miraculous, tells
us what sounds like a parable. The Saint's party arrive,
weary from their journey. The King, proud and haughty,
disdains to open his gates. So the Saint

[1] III, 4.

came with his companions to the doors in the gates, traced on them the sign of the cross, knocked, laid his hand upon the doors, and they flew open of their own accord, and in he went with his company.[1]

Demythologize as you will, it must have been some spiritual force which gained the entry and made on the King such an impression that 'he honoured the holy and venerable man all the rest of his life, which [adds Adamnan] was right and proper'.

What of their missionary method? Adamnan says that Columba 'often sent away the heathen priests abashed, and vanquished by him'[2], perhaps referring to preaching against heathen superstition. The illustration which he gives is of dramatic action, the public and purposeful breaking of a taboo, to prove such superstition false. The scene was a spring, at which no one dared drink or wash.

Men said that doing so one might be struck with leprosy, or blindness, or be made feeble, or ailing in some way. And so, misguided as they were, they worshipped the spirit of the spring... The Saint went up. He raised his holy hand and called upon the name of Christ. Then he washes hands and feet, and with his companions drinks of the water he has blessed. . . . The demons from that day disappeared, and not only was no one hurt there any more, but the spring became a place where people were healed.

There are four accounts of conversion and baptism. Two of them remind us of the Acts of the Apostles.

While the Saint was in Pictland for several days, he preached through an interpreter. One man, hearing the word, *believed and was baptized with all his family*, wife, children, and servants.[3]

In the other two cases, baptism is sought by a man of good character on the approach of death.

When the Saint was staying for some days in Skye . . . a boat

[1] II, 35.   [2] II, 11.
[3] II, 32; also III, 14; compare Acts 18.8, etc.

C

arrived with an aged Pict, chieftain of his tribe, in its bows, and two youths who lifted him out . . . . And he received the word through an interpreter, and believed and was baptized.[1]

He died soon after.

There is no suggestion of a mass movement, a tribal chief bringing the whole community with him. Because they are lone individuals, these two wait till life is almost over before they can break with pagan society. One of these families, because it stands alone, soon has its faith sorely tried. A son of the house dies, and the pagan priests step in and say that this is the price of leaving the old gods, who are stronger than the God of the Christians. As Adamnan tells the story, the dead boy is raised. His remark that Columba thus stands with the prophets Elijah and Elisha (I Kings 17; II Kings 4), and the apostles Peter and Paul (Acts 9 and 20), may make the critic wonder if the biblical incidents suggested the happy ending. The incident itself, however, a newly converted family sorely tried, is not paralleled in any of the four biblical accounts. It can be paralleled in the experience of any missionary.

We may include another incident as Christian preaching, since Christian worship is one of the best means of Christian witness. The Saint once, 'with a few of his brethren', sang the evening Office outside the castle of King Brude.

> The heathen priests did all they could to keep the sound of divine praise from being heard by their people. When the Saint knew this, he began to chant Psalm 45, and in a wonderful way his voice was caught up into the air like thunder, aweing both King and people.[2]

Adamnan says that Columba had a marvellous voice, and sometimes each syllable could be heard a mile away. He adds whimsically,

> It did not always happen, but that it happened at all was only by grace of God's Spirit.

[1] I, 33; also III, 14.   [2] I, 37.

On this occasion the Latin syllables of Psalm 45 may have been lost on the hearers.

> Gird thy sword upon thy thigh, O most mighty,
> with thy glory and thy majesty.
> And in thy majesty ride prosperously,
> because of truth and meekness and righteousness.

But the singers would think of their Lord's triumphal entry into another city. And who knows? Their singing may have been one of the keys which opened the doors of the castle.

What was Christianity's appeal? In the baptism of the two who were dying we may see, as in so many cases (p. 93), the appeal of a religion which has a message of life beyond death.

There are traces of medical work. A man comes to Iona 'shouting across the Sound' (of Mull), seeking medical aid.[1] On missionary journeys, as any missionary's experience will suggest, they could hardly avoid doing something to relieve the sick.

Did they have educational work? Columba had to preach through an interpreter. With Saxons and a Briton among the monks, were there Picts as well, learning to be priests to their own people? Bede tells that when Aidan, trained at Iona, came to Northumbria, one of his first acts was to found a school for training English boys for the priesthood (p. 100). Adamnan mentions Columba's pupils, but does not say whether there were Picts among them.

For people who were Christians, but far from any monastery and without a local church, the wandering missionary must have been the one chance to receive the Church's ministrations. A child was presented for baptism 'as the Saint passed through Ardnamurchan [northern Argyll], where to this day there is a health-giving well called by St Columba's name'. Adamnan believed the reason to be that the water bubbled up in answer to his prayer, but 'sacred' springs and wells were common among

[1] I, 25.

the heathen, and we may believe that this became sacred in a new way by its Christian use.[1]

We have one surprising picture of the Saint engaged in marriage guidance, when he was staying on Rathlin Island —but it might have happened anywhere. Lugne, a peasant, complains that his wife will not let him come to her. To Columba the woman says, 'I will do all the housework. I will cross the sea and enter a nunnery if you say so. But I will not live with Lugne as wife.' So far from encouraging her to be a nun, the Saint says, 'Let us three spend the day in fasting and prayer.' For his part, he adds to the day a sleepless night, praying for them. Next morning he asks the woman, 'What about the nunnery now?' 'God must have heard your prayer', she says. 'My heart this past night has changed from hate to love.'[2]

If, as Bede says, Columba was the converter of the Northern Picts, he can only have begun their conversion. But he had one completed work among his own people, the Scots of Dalriada. After the death of his kinsman Conall, their King, in 574, Columba decided which of the family should succeed.

> The Saint obeyed the word of the Lord, and sailed [from Hinba where this 'word' came to him] to Iona, Aidan coming at the same time. And there, as he had been commanded, Columba consecrated Aidan as King. . . . laying his hands upon his head and blessing him.[3]

Aidan was a Christian already. Columba's mission, among these Scottish settlers, in what is now Argyll, was not so much to plant Christianity as to confirm it. Columba's act marks the Scottish monarchy's *Christian* re-beginning, and marks the recognition of the Iona monastery as the Mother Church of Scottish Christianity.

Adamnan mentions Columba's having two things which are often associated with a Celtic saint, and which in some cases have been preserved—a staff and a bell. I have hand-

[1] II, 10.   [2] II, 41.   [3] III, 5.

led 'the bachul (Latin, *baculum*) of St Moluag', preserved at Lismore, near Oban, which he made his island base, while Columba was working from Iona. It is a branch of blackthorn, three feet long, bent at the top, the staff of the wandering missionary.[1] We have noticed Columba's bell (p. 58). A quadrangular handbell, thought to have been his, I have also handled, in the Museum of National Antiquities, Edinburgh. I wanted to ring it, to hear the sound that called men, not only in Iona, but when the Saint was on tour, the summons of the missionary. But after fourteen centuries parts are rusted away, and, alas, the block of wood, inside to support it, makes it dumb.

Columba comes closest, and most real, in the ending of Adamnan's book which he entitles, 'The passing to the Lord of our holy Father'.[2] Could anyone have kept such a vivid memory but Diormit himself? Though needing to abbreviate, I will stick close to Adamnan's words.

In May of the year 597 he knew that the end was near, and wanted to see again his monks at work in the fields, so they drove him round in an ox-cart. There in the fertile western plain, he faced east, and blessed the island and its people. No poisonous snake, nor any harmful beast, has since been seen. At the Sunday Mass, on June 2nd, they noticed his face aglow. One of them asked what he had seen.

An angel, come to fetch something dear to God. And, after looking down upon us and blessing us, he has gone, and left it, for just a little while.

On the next Saturday (June 8th) he crossed to the barn and blessed it. And there he told the sorrowing Diormit his secret, that this day was to see his Sabbath rest. Going out, he sat down weary, half-way to his hut, where now, says Adamnan, a cross set in a mill-stone marks the place. The faithful old white horse, which carried the milk pails, came up, put his head on the Saint's arm, and began to whinny. He said to Diormit,

[1] I, 33; II, 14.   [2] III, 23.

Let be. You I had to tell about my passing, but this dumb beast knows from God himself.

And so he blessed his servant the horse.

Back in his hut, he went on copying a Psalter, till he came to Psalm 34.10,' 'They that seek the Lord shall not want any good thing'. 'There', he said, 'I must stop. The rest let Baithene write.' Baithene was to succeed him. When the bell rang for midnight prayers, he was up and into the church even before they had brought the lights. Diormit went in, calling, 'Where are you, Father?' He groped and found him, lying before the altar. He lifted the Saint's head on his arm, as the brethren came in with lights, and stood round weeping. And those present say that he looked round upon them all, on one side, then the other, with joy most wonderful. Diormit lifted the Saint's right hand that he might bless them, and the Saint moved it to make the sign of the cross, as he was able. And so his spirit departed.

His face had flushed with joy when he saw the angels' coming and so it remained, not like one taken in death, but just left sleeping.

About the beginning of the Church in what was then becoming Scotland, there is much that we do not know. But we do know one man. And of him we know one thing supremely. How they loved him!

IV

The Southern Roman Mission

BEDE SAYS that the Apostle of England is Pope Gregory himself.

> While as Pope he ruled all Christendom . . . it was he who made our nation, till then given up to idols, into a Church of Christ.[1]

And then, quoting with only a change of pronouns I Corinthians 9.2 he continues,

> If he be not an apostle unto others, yet he is to us, for the seal of his apostleship are we in the Lord.

Gregory's first interest in Britain is well known, the incident, before he was Pope, of fair-headed slaves in the market-place in Rome.

> Of what nation? Angles! They have faces of angels. Of what province? Deira [Yorkshire]! They shall be saved *de ira* [from wrath].
> And their king? Aella! Then must Alleluia be sung in that land.

Many, familiar with this from childhood, may not realize that it has a place, not only in that first history reader, but in this same chapter of the Venerable Bede. Gregory seems to have been given to such play upon words. An eighth-century *Life of Gregory* by a monk of Whitby goes on to say that he got the Pope's permission to go himself as missionary to the English, but was stopped on the third day. A grasshopper settled on his open book and he exclaimed, '*Locusta*

[1] *Ecclesiastical History*, II, 1.

—that means *loco sta* (stand still in the place). We shall not be able to go on.' A message recalling him soon came. A crowd had demonstrated on his departure, chanting as they advanced on St Peter's a jingle which expressed the city's need for its capable ecclesiastic:

> Gregory send,
> Peter offend,
> And Rome end.

Bede, though he does not record the incident, does say, 'The people of Rome would not let him go.'

Oral tradition is full of puns (and jingles) because they are aids to memory, so naturally they often come to be included in written records. But the same play on words occurs in Gregory's own letters. Writing to the Patriarch of Alexandria about Augustine's mission, he says, 'The Angles, set in an angle (*angulo*) of the world. . . .' To him this was more than punning. He saw an omen in a name. Above all, he used this play upon words to give point to his statements. We see the point, for we remember after fourteen centuries.

Gregory was born of a patrician family in Rome about the year 540. A church and monastery dedicated to him now stand upon the site of his home, the foundations, court after court of the great house, being visible in the cellars of these buildings. It looked towards the Palatine Hill, with all its associations of imperial glory, and present signs of imperial decay. The Emperor Justinian's re-conquest of the west had been wholly disastrous for Italy. The Gothic peace was exchanged for twenty-seven years (535-562) of war, looting, famine, and crushing taxation. Now Italy might be claimed as 'Roman' again, but the Emperor's occupying troops were more alien than the Goths had been, and Italy never recovered from her liberation. Rome had endured five sieges. It was left a city of crumbling buildings, broken aqueducts, grass-grown courts. Its one sign of life was that churches were being enlarged and adorned, and one, that of the Holy Apostles, was newly built, a spacious basilica with murals and mosaics. Rome, the capital of the Republic and the Empire, had passed away. Rome's sole glory would be as capital of the Church.

Gregory's education suffered from the ills of the times, but he acquired a workmanlike written style, and a distinguished spoken one, was well trained in law, and gifted musically. His Christian upbringing owed much to this city of churches, but most to his devout home. He looked, as his family had done, to the public service. Men of rank, wealth, education, and piety were few in Rome then. Small wonder that, at the age of thirty-two, Gregory had become Civil Governor (*Praefectus*) of the city. He presided over the Senate, a shadow of its former self, saw to the city's jurisdiction, officials, finances, was consulted by the military commander about its defence, and by the Pope about its relief. If Rome's decay subtracted from the glamour of the office, decadence, prevailing poverty, and threats of Lombard invasion, added to its burdens.

The happening of the year 574 is not surprising. 'The world passeth away and the lusts thereof.' That text was writ large over what had been the world's capital. Gregory had by now inherited his father's vast estate. He decided to give it all to the poor, and to the founding of seven monasteries, one, dedicated to St Andrew, in the great house which had been his home. And there he would still live, exchanging the silk robes of his high office for the coarse gown of the monk. Gregory later writes as if the next five years of ascetic contemplation were the time of his deepest spiritual content. One wonders. There were two Gregories, as there are two sides to most of us. Those who twice called Gregory from the monastery were not wrong in seeing that here was a man of action. The first call was in 579, when the Pope appointed him Seventh Deacon. These seven corresponded to the divisions of the city, and were set, somewhat like archdeacons, over its churches. But they were also consultants for the Pope. Soon the Seventh

Deacon was sent as Papal Envoy (*Apocrisiarius*) to the court of Constantinople, for seven years.

On his return he was elected Abbot of St Andrew's monastery, and with joy took up again the quiet life of what was both the home of his childhood and his spiritual home. We may assume that the incident of the market-place falls within this period, 586-590. It was in the year 590 that the second call came.

Plague had swept through Italy, and brought the stillness of death to Rome. The Pope was among the victims. There was no doubt among either clergy or people of Rome with regard to his successor. Gregory's whole life had been preparation for this—first, governor of Rome, then devoted monk, then diplomat in the eastern capital, now outstanding among the late Pope's most intimate advisers. He was nominated by the clergy and acclaimed by the people. His election lacked only confirmation by the Emperor.

Yet Gregory hesitated. Within that same experience which we have labelled preparation lay reasons for doubt. He had grown up in a falling world; would there be time for the vast reforms which he saw the Church needed? He had fled from the world's glory; as Pope, would world-liness, insidiously disguised, creep on him again? He was even then writing a book, *The Pastoral Rule*, about the spiritual gifts required for the Bishop's office; to think that one could fulfil that office in St Peter's holy See might be pride, the sin of Lucifer. So one part of Gregory wanted to withdraw, and he wrote to tell the Emperor so.

But Gregory's other self knew that it had to be. In reply to congratulations from the Patriarch of Constantinople, he wrote that it was like

> being called to the command of an old battered ship, leaking all over, its timbers rotten, shaken every day by storms, sound-ing of wreck.

Answering the Bishop of Corinth, he wrote,

> I wished to be free of this burden. . . . I might fail in the

Pastoral Rule. . . . But one cannot resist what God has ordained.

His years at Constantinople had convinced him that the Emperor there had nothing he could do for western Europe. It was for the Pope to do something. He proceeded to make Rome once more the place to which all western Christians looked—people of the older stocks, and immigrant populations alike, Visigoths in Spain, Franks in Gaul, Lombards in North Italy, the mixed populations of North Africa— not now for an Emperor, but towards that Bishop who was 'Servant of the servants of God'.

It is as *our* Apostle, and that alone, that here we must regard him. We must look at his founding of the mission, its beginnings in Kent, the policies which he recommended, and the measure in which they were carried out.

Pope Gregory's first move towards a mission to the English was in 595, and again was associated with the slave-market. He wrote to a priest in Gaul telling him to buy some English boys seventeen to eighteen years old. We hear no more of this. He must have come to realize that their training, even for a minor part, would take years, and he had a sense of urgency. Would there be time? He writes this in a letter to Gaul:

> News has reached us that the people of the English look and long (*desideranter velle*) to be converted to the Christian faith, but priests from nearby do not bother.

The opportunity of which he heard lay, not in Deira, but indeed 'nearby' to Gaul, in Kent. Bede speaks of its king as

> the powerful Ethelbert who had extended his rule north to the river Humber. . . . He had heard something of the Christian religion, having a Christian wife of the Frankish royal house.[1]

This was Gregory's chance. He showed his concern for the mission by sending the man who was Prior (under himself, still Abbot) of St Andrew's Monastery—Augustine. Later

[1] I, 25.

there were forty monks, but some had joined the party in Gaul. They sailed in the spring of 596.

Bede says,

> On their way they were struck with a sudden fear, and thought of going back home. . . . They all agreed it were safer so.[1]

Evidently they heard what fierce folk these Saxons were, and, in a foreign land already, realized how lost they would be without the language. So Augustine left them in South Gaul and went to ask the Pope to release them from this task. Instead, Gregory wrote back a letter which begins,

> Gregory, Servant of the servants of God, to those who serve our Lord. Better not to set out on the right way than, having set out, to think of turning back.

The harder the labour, the greater will be the reward. Indeed he hopes that when he himself is in heaven he will see the fruits of their labours and share the reward, as he would gladly have shared in the mission. He sends Augustine back as their Abbot—which means that he can demand their obedience without further reference to himself. They must take Frankish interpreters to Kent. At the same time he wrote to several Bishops of Gaul to ask them to set them on their journey, and to powerful laymen, including the boy-kings of Austrasia (the Eastern Franks) and Burgundy, and their formidable grandmother, Brunhild.

Here, since we rely so constantly on Bede, we may notice one thing about him. Ancient and medieval historians have a way of making up speeches and putting them into the mouths of their characters. They do similarly with letters. And rightly so. It is a historian's duty not only to record but to interpret. But one must be careful not to accept such words as more than interpretation, as being a man's own. Here we need not hesitate. Bede wrote everywhere for copies of documents. Of the Pope's letter to Augustine he writes, 'The gist of his letter was . . .' and then gives 155

[1] I, 23.

words of it. He would get a copy either from the Abbot of the monastery at Canterbury, or from Nothelm, a London priest, later (735) Archbishop of Canterbury, who, visiting Rome, worked for Bede among the Papal archives.

The journey of these monks of St Andrew's across Gaul, so full of historical associations, was good preparation for the writing of this new chapter of church history. They travelled by way of Marseilles, where in 415 John Cassian founded his monastery, one of the first to bring so far westward the ways of the Desert Fathers. Then on to Arles, where, at the synod of 314, Bishops from Britain first appeared. Then to Lyons, where in 177 Bishop Pothinus and 47 of his flock died as martyrs, and Irenaeus lived to succeed him, Irenaeus, through Polycarp a link with the Apostles, through preaching to the Celts a link with Britain too (p. 14). And so to Reims, where Clovis and three thousand of his warriors were baptized in 496 (p. 47); and Tours, where St Martin died in 397 while St Ninian's *Candida Casa* was building (p. 31). They were hospitably received by the ruler of Paris, and so wintered among the Franks. Soon after Easter they crossed the Channel.[1]

They landed at Richborough, where the River Stour comes winding into Pegwell Bay, between Ramsgate and Sandwich. Not much of a river, it is flanked by marshes, with marshland in those days extending across to Reculver on Kent's north coast, making the Isle of Thanet really an island. Bede never in his life travelled farther than York, but he got all the details: 'fordable only in two places', is what he says. They sent to King Ethelbert, telling him that they had come from Rome,

> bringing good news of everlasting joy in heaven, and a kingdom that knows no end, with the true and living God.

The King told them to stay where they were till he decided on their case.

We can see what was in his mind. Foreigners are to be

[1] Bede's account proceeds now from I, 25 on.

treated with care, especially from that awe-inspiring city of Rome. Priests of another faith are better at a distance, for who knows the power of their gods? True, he has a Christian wife, with her chaplain, Liudhard, and no harm as yet. But here are Christians out to get him. Good news, is it? Fear of another's magic is a kind of claustrophobia, and Ethelbert decided to give them an audience in the open. 'But theirs', says the wise Bede,

> was not magic but the power of God. They came with a silver cross as their standard, and on a board a picture of our Lord and Saviour. And as they came they sang a litany, and offered prayers for their own salvation and for the people to whom they were come.

Notice the 'visual aid'. Pope Gregory may have suggested it. These are words of his from another context:

> Pictures are used in churches so that those who are illiterate might at least read by looking at the walls,

> Pictures are to the illiterate what books are to educated men.

Ethelbert proved favourable:

> Your words are fair, your promises good. But to us it is all new and untried. I cannot agree so far as to break with all that I so long have followed with all the people of the English. But since you come from far, if I understand aright, especially to pass on what you believe to be true and beneficial, we will not molest you, but entertain you, and provide for your needs. Nor do we forbid you to preach and gain converts for your religion.

So a house was assigned to them in Canterbury, his capital, and this time Bede gives the words of the litany they sang, as the same procession—silver cross, painting of Christ, Augustine and his forty monks—entered the city:

> We beseech thee, O Lord, in thy mercy that thine anger and wrath be turned away from this city and from thy holy house, for we have sinned (Dan. 9.16).

A litany requires response, and the response here was 'Alleluia!'

Augustine soon went off, as Pope Gregory had instructed him, to Arles, for the Archbishop there to consecrate him. On his return he sent messengers to Rome to tell of his good beginning, to request reinforcements, and to ask nine questions. They seem paltry questions for one engaged in founding a new province of the Church:

1. How does a bishop behave to his clergy and in church, and to what purposes does one allocate the offerings?
2. Why are there differences in the liturgy, e.g. in Rome and Gaul?
3. How should robbers of churches be punished?
4 and 5. What are the forbidden degrees with regard to marriage?
6. Can a bishop be consecrated by a single bishop?
7. How should he deal with the bishops of Gaul and of the Britons?
8 and 9. Are baptism, church attendance, and communion, allowed during pregnancy, and in cases of female and male 'uncleanness', as dealt with in Leviticus 15?

We shall notice the mission's further progress as we consider questions of missionary policy amd method.

First comes the question of group conversion. Professor K. S. Latourette says of this period,

> Conversion became not so much a matter of individual conviction as of group action, a marked departure from the original nature of Christianity, and from the usual processes of expansion in the first three centuries. It was conformity to what seems to have been, until the time of Christ, a prevailing conception of religion . . . as a tribal or national affair.[1]

Latourette omits one crucial factor. It is the structure of society, rather than the preference of the missionary, which decides whether the response is to be by individuals or by the group. For example, David Livingstone, a Congre-

[1] *Expansion of Christianity*, II, 16.

gationalist, took with him to Africa the principles of 'the gathered Church . . . the worthiest, be they never so few' —the very antithesis of 'religion as a tribal or national affair'. Yet everywhere his first approach was to the chief of the tribe. In a tribal society you cannot approach people one by one. The tribe is the unit, and, instead of disrupting society, the wise way is to try to influence it as a whole through its headmen.

Latourette speaks of 'departure from the processes of expansion in the first three centuries'. Christianity in the Roman Empire was launched into a society uniquely cosmopolitan and individualist. From the fifth century on, as we have seen, that was passing. For many, life was returning to something nearer to tribal conditions, not cosmopolitan and individualist, but local and feudal. Such a community was likely to decide together. The conversion of our ancestors was a change of community religion.

Many have criticized this. The prevalence today of a merely nominal Christianity is put down to this 'mass movement' acceptance of the faith. But why bewail Christianity's becoming our community religion? One clergyman complains, 'I answered the call to the Church's service, as being related to causes which make front-page news; generally I seem to be relegated to the columns for births, marriages, and deaths.'

Now religion all over the world is like that. Most people are not very religious. They turn to religion in the crises of life—births, marriages and deaths. But is it not a true advance when the religion turned to is the religion of the God and Father of our Lord Jesus Christ? And are not these crises the clergy's recurring opportunity to bring men once and for all to knowledge of him?

The Christianity of our ancestors began in group conversion. It is not much good having an opinion for or against this method. It was inevitable, from the structure of society. The Church too had changed its condition since the first three centuries. No longer the minority, the sect saved out of the world, at war with the world, it had become the imperial state Church, central in society, and influencing the world's life. When the Empire passed in the west, the Church maintained its claim to a central place, remained central among the new peoples of Europe, as through the travail of the Dark Ages these nations came to birth.

Second, we must examine the means of approach. This is through some influential Christian, most often a Christian queen. Women's tremendous place in religion all over the world is not unconnected with the fact that in the crises of births, marriages, and deaths, women are the chief actors. I have elsewhere written of women's major part in the spread of Christianity in the first three centuries.[1] We have seen the influence of Clotilda behind the baptism of Clovis (p. 47), and remarked that Bertha, her great-grand-daughter, would open the door to Pope Gregory's missionaries. Soon we shall see Bertha's daughter, married to King Edwin, doing the same in Northumbria. Pope Gregory expected much from Christian women in high places. He wrote to the Dowager Brunhild about assisting the conversion of heathen among the Franks. He constantly got what he wanted (chiefly toleration for Catholics) by correspondence with Theodelinda, the Catholic wife of the Arian Lombard King. Women's influence was so often used by Gregory that he came to think of it as the norm. This rubric and charge before the crowning of a Queen may come from him:

A ring is to be put on her finger. 'Receive this as token of faith in the holy Trinity, by which you may be able to shun every taint of heresy, and, by maintenance of your goodness, call barbarian peoples to the knowledge of the truth.'[2]

Pope Gregory had seen it happen so often.

Third, we must enquire about methods of evangelism.

At first the monks from Rome preached through inter-

---

[1] *After the Apostles*, pp. 38-45.
[2] *The Gregorian Sacramentary*, p. 285.

preters, the Franks who accompanied them from Gaul. As for subject, the only hint we have is in the 'visual aid' which we noticed. The picture of Christ was probably the crucifixion. The subject, then, was 'Christ and him crucified'. Given permission by the King to preach among his subjects, Bede says, 'They became like the primitive Church.' So they were, except for persecution, a small minority, alien to the life of this heathen kingdom. He goes on:

> They gave themselves to prayer, watching, and fasting. They preached to as many as they could. They despised all worldly things as not belonging to them. They accepted only their food from those they taught, and lived in all respects as they preached, ready to suffer, and, if need be, to die for the faith, And so several believed and were baptized. . . .

Several! Not many as yet—this was a minority movement.

> On the east side of the city was a church, built when the Romans were in the land, dedicated to St Martin, which the Queen used for prayer. In this church they began to meet, to sing, to say mass, to preach, and to baptize.

Bede goes on to tell of the difference when Ethelbert was baptized, on June 1st, Whitsun Eve. I like the way he mentions the King's conversion: 'When, among the rest, he believed and was baptized . . . . ' It was a real conversion, with no conditions made, such as Clovis's prayer for victory over his enemies. Nor was it part of a general adoption of Roman ways; there was little of that as yet. He had chosen to leave the gods of his fathers for the God of his wife, and of these missionaries. Bede continues,

> Then greater numbers began to come together to hear the word and to forsake their heathen ways and join the Church. The King was known to be pleased at their faith and conversion, not that he would drive anyone to the Christian fold, for those who prepared him for baptism had taught him that one must choose to serve Christ, not be forced to it. But it was known that he would show more liking to believers, as fellow-citizens of the kingdom of heaven.

Gregory once wrote—about bringing Jews to the faith, but he would instruct Augustine similarly—

> Bring a man to baptism by compulsion instead of by consent, and you may expect to find him fall away.

The Pope joyfully passed the news to the Patriarch of Alexandria that on Christmas Day, 597, more than ten thousand were baptized near the mouth of the River Medway. The mission had indeed begun to result in a mass movement to the Christian faith.

Fourth, we must consider policy for developing an English Church.

The Pope showed himself a missionary-statesman in three respects.

(1) The English mission was started with a well-thought-out plan. It looked to nothing less than the conversion of the whole country—and that long before the country *was* whole, divided into several petty kingdoms. One thinks of cases in the modern missionary movement where planning on such a scale came only after 100 to 120 years of local muddling. In 601 came reinforcements, led by Mellitus (later Bishop of London), and with them these instructions. Augustine was made Archbishop and told to consecrate twelve bishops for his Province. He was to send a bishop to York, hoping for him to become Archbishop there with a Province of twelve bishops too.[1] It was to be about 900 years before the Church in England was divided into so many dioceses, but such was the line of its development. Far-sighted indeed, this missionary statesman!

(2) Provision was made for the development of an English 'use' (local modification of the liturgy). This is implied in the Pope's answer to Augustine's second question:

> If you have found anything, either in the Roman, Gallican, or any other Church, which may be more acceptable to almighty God, carefully make choice of the same, and pass on to the Church of the English, which as yet is new in the faith, what-

[1] I, 29.

ever you can gather from the several Churches. For things are not to be loved for the sake of places, but places for the good things in them.[1]

Again we may remark upon the foresight which from the outset assumed something more than reproduction of the ways of their home church.

(3) The mission was to be accommodating to English ways. Gregory first demanded that heathen temples should be destroyed, but he wrote to Mellitus about a different policy. Destroy idols, he said, but sprinkle the temple with holy water, furnish it with altar and relics, and—provided it is well built—dedicate it as a church.

Thus the people will more readily come to places to which they have been accustomed.[2]

He hears that there are times when the English sacrifice many cattle. He means the autumn slaughter, for lack of winter fodder. Let them keep this custom, camping in huts of tree-branches round the temple, now become a church. But let the feasting be associated no longer with sacrifice to devils, but with thanksgiving to God—a dedication, or a festival of the martyr whose relics they have. Animal sacrifice in the Old Testament he regards as a stage in Israel's progress, and adds, 'He who would mount to the highest place must go up by steps and strides, not by leaps'. While the emphasis is upon accommodation, this attempt to baptize local custom into Christian use does make towards a measure of indigenous expression.

Where did Gregory get the idea? Some say from Augustine. He had already taken over a former church, desecrated by heathen worship, and re-consecrated it, the church of St Pancras. I suggest that more important was the example of the first two illustrious Gregories of church history. Gregory the Wonder-worker (213-270) was missionary-bishop in Pontus and under him the first Christian mass-movement took place. He used his knowledge of local custom to replace pagan feasts by festivals of the martyrs, of the Decian persecution just passed. A mass-movement under Gregory the Enlightener (240-332) brought Armenia to be the first nation to make Christianity its national religion. Pope Gregory would know these saints to whom he was namesake and he was following them.

What was done on these lines? Here and there one finds a church set on a tumulus, or by a standing stone, or where there was once a stone circle. Some sacred sites would have no building—a tree, a well or spring, a hill, a forest clearing, and we know many a church where the place-name bears such a meaning. But how many temples would come up to Gregory's specification, well built? Gregory's knowledge was of Rome, but the early English built in wood.

A last word about Augustine himself. He seems to have been unimaginative and overbearing. Unimaginative—he did not realize until he had set out that it would be dangerous, and that he would need a foreign language. He did not know elementary rulings of the Church about sex. Can a man marry his stepmother? he asks; can a pregnant woman be baptized? To the latter, the Pope replies, Why not? Where had he been till middle-age? When he knew he was to be a missionary-bishop, why did he not catch up on his pastoralia, instead of waiting until he was consecrated?

And overbearing. A senior colleague of mine, who on retirement gave one year to service in one of the younger Churches, speaking of some missionaries asked me, 'Why do apostles become autocrats?' The answer must be that both are made of the same stuff—apostleship requires a forceful personality. In Augustine's case there are three signs of weakness here. The letter from the Pope in 601 dwells on the danger of pride.

I know that God has wrought miracles through you. Rejoice, but with fear, trembling as you rejoice. What do I mean? Rejoice because by outward miracles there may come to the English something of inward grace. Tremble lest, because of the wonders wrought, you may be puffed up. Remember that the Twelve returned with joy saying, 'Lord, even the devils are subject to us', and he said, 'Rejoice rather that your names are written in heaven'. And so it is for you to judge yourself strictly, and know yourself . . . to keep in mind your own shortcomings in word and deed, and set them over against any tendency towards pride.[1]

Perhaps better than holding this against Augustine would be recollection of how often we ourselves have needed a wise father-in-God like that, in times of prosperity, even of success in Christ's service.

There is evidence of self-assertion behind Augustine's seventh question (p. 79), how should he deal with the bishops of Gaul. The Pope forcefully replies that Augustine has no jurisdiction there, that the Bishop of Arles is Archbishop of that province, and if Augustine wishes to correct them it can only be by a good example.

The British bishops were also mentioned, and over them the Pope did give him authority. Bede gives an account of the sequel, the conference at St Augustine's Oak, thought to have been Aust on the southern bank of the Severn. He tells of a hermit's advice to the British bishops:

'If he is a man of God, follow him.'—'How shall we know?' 'Our Lord said, "I am meek and lowly of heart". If he is meek and lowly, he may bear the yoke of Christ.'—'But how shall we know?' 'Let him arrive first. When you come in, if he rise up to greet you, hear him submissively. If not, he despises you, and I say, despise you him.'[2]

He did not rise up. As that ancient handbell has been passed down, believed to be Columba's, so on oak chair stands in the church of Stamford Bishop, Herefordshire, as the one in which Augustine sat. A missionary would prefer a bell as his relic.[3]

Why do apostles become autocrats? I have rejected the late legend which turns Columba into a man of violence, but a masterful man he surely was. Yet anyone reading

[1] I, 31.   [2] II, 2.

[3] In 1850 the old sexton said that he had it from his predecessors that the chair used to stand in the chancel as St Augustine's. It is undoubtedly most ancient.

Adamnan must say, as I said, 'How they loved him!' There is little of this in what has come down about Augustine. It may be the sources, but one suspects it is the subject which is different—which is less.

What Augustine achieved was less than Pope Gregory had hoped. He was probably less adventurous in development of Church and liturgy than the Pope had encouraged him to be. But his was a great achievement. He had started the mission in Kent, and become first Archbishop of Canterbury, with bishops at London and Rochester. He had converted a King, and begun the conversion of a kingdom. He had established a Province, and linked this island with the centre of Christendom from which he had come.

V

The Conversion of Northumbria

PAULINUS OF YORK, 625
AIDAN OF LINDISFARNE, 635

BEDE'S MOST vivid material concerns the conversion of his
own Northumbria. Although separated from the events by
a full century, he even got, from the Abbot of Partney (in
Lincolnshire), a picture of Paulinus the missionary, as he
was remembered by one of his converts

> baptized, with a crowd of others, in the presence of King
> Edwin, at midday in the River Trent, by a tall man with a
> stoop, black hair, a lean look, a nose hooked and thin, and
> a presence inspiring reverence and awe.[1]

Doubtless he got other memories from

> James the Deacon, with him in this ministry, a man of in-
> dustry and renown, who lived on to our own times.

He shows us not only the missionary but the mission, its
opportunities and how they were taken, the appeal of the
new religion, the needs it met, and the way it was pro-
claimed. He traces Christian influences over King Edwin's
youth, apparently from Kent by way of East Anglia;
influences strengthened and consummated by Ethelburga,
his Kentish Christian wife; and his own thoughtful progress
to full personal conviction. He gives us two contrasting
pictures from among Edwin's advisers. First comes the
chief-priest Coifi, with his mercenary cynicism about the
gods, 'What good have they ever done to me?'—until the
preaching of Paulinus brings him to a position positive
enough for him to desecrate and set fire to his own temple.
On the other hand is the pathetic questioning of the noble-

[1] II, 6.

man,—'Whence do I come? Why am I here? Whither do I go?'—surely the heart-cry of true religion. With regard to the common people, he shows us systematic hard work at catechizing, and baptisms at the riverside. So first to the King!

If the attempt to establish in Britain a northern province of the Church was not, as Pope Gregory had hoped, begun by Augustine, it did happen in a way familiar to that Pope, and which, had he been still alive, would have had his blessing. In 625, Ethelburga, daughter of Queen Bertha of Kent, repeated the experience of her mother, and was asked for in marriage by a non-Christian King. Her brother Eadbald, now King of Kent, replied to the suitor, Edwin, King of Northumbria, that the Church would forbid such a marriage.

> But Edwin declared it possible that he might himself submit to her religion, provided that his wise men (Witan) should find it holier and more worthy of God. And so the maid was promised, and sent to Edwin. And, as had been arranged, Paulinus, a man dear to God, was ordained bishop to go with her, to strengthen her and her companions against the defilement of mixing with the heathen, by daily exhortation and celebration of the blessed sacrament.[1]

Why had Edwin looked to Kent, and why had he been so ready to contemplate Christian conversion? Bede seems to provide the clues, without himself bringing the evidence together. Perhaps he never asked these questions. He tells the story of a mysterious visitant ten years before. Edwin had then been a fugitive, finding refuge in the territory of Redwald, King of the East Anglians. Aethelfrith, King of Northumbria, bribed and threatened Redwald into agreeing to betray Edwin into his hands. A stranger appeared to Edwin with three offers: deliverance from his enemies, a kingdom greater than that of any of his forbears, and, in addition, a salvation to them unknown, if he would promise to obey. He promised. The stranger then

[1] II, 9.

placed his right hand on Edwin's head, saying, 'When this sign shall be given you, remember, and keep your word'.[1]

It was Redwald's Queen who saved Edwin's life, by protesting to her husband against his plan to betray him. In another passage Bede tells us that the same Queen had earlier protested against her husband's conversion to Christianity while he was in Kent, and persuaded him to compromise.[2] He did set up in a temple an altar to Christ, but he kept a side-altar, says Bede, 'for sacrifices to devils, like the Samaritans of old' (II Kings 17.41). In 616 Edwin was delivered from his enemies. In 617 Northumbria, stretching now from the Humber to the Forth, had become his kingdom. What of the third promise? In Redwald's kingdom he had met Christianity of a kind, and learned to associate it with Kent. He may well have suspected the mysterious stranger to be a Christian. When in 625 he looked to Kent for a bride he already had the idea that her religion might be one 'holier and more worthy of God'.

Three decisive happenings came in the evening and night after Easter Day of the year 626. First, one pretending to bring him a message from the King of Wessex, brought instead a poisoned sword. Edwin's one attendant saw him draw, and, being unarmed and without a shield, flung himself in front of the King. So fierce was the thrust that it ran him through, and wounded the King beyond. Second, the Queen gave birth to a daughter. And third,

When the King, in Bishop Paulinus' presence, gave thanks to his gods, the Bishop began thanksgiving to the Lord Christ, adding, 'It was I who obtained of Christ by my prayers that your Lady the Queen should have her child without difficult labour.' The King was pleased at this and promised, 'I will renounce the idols and serve Christ if he will give me my life, and victory in the fight with that King who sent the murderer and wounded me, in pledge of which I give my little daughter to be consecrated to Christ by you.' She was ac-

[1] II, 12.   [2] II, 15.

cordingly christened at Pentecost, firstfruit of the Northumbrian people, with eleven more of her family.[1]

Edwin's wound did heal with no poisoning. His punitive expedition to Wessex was victorious. He was now so far committed that he broke with idol-worship, but his steps towards the font were slow, because, unlike Redwald, he knew that baptism meant a complete break with the past.

He was careful, as occasion offered, to receive instruction from Paulinus on the grounds of the Faith, as well as to take counsel with the wiser of his chiefs, what it were best to do. He was naturally a thoughtful man, and often sat alone, his lips silent but his inmost heart asking so many questions, 'What must I do? Which religion ought I to follow?'

Then came two letters from Pope Boniface, one to Edwin, and one to Ethelburga. They must have been long delayed, as the Pope had died the previous December. That to Edwin is of value as a sample—and we have not many—of something like missionary preaching.

God [he says] is beyond words to describe him, beyond what thought can conceive. Yet he has given man some knowledge of himself, even this gospel which our Saviour commanded us to preach to all nations. God is creator of heaven and earth and sea, and of all that is in them. Man, made of dust, but in God's image, he has set over all creation, and made capable of receiving eternal life. God, Father, Son, and Holy Spirit, is thus confessed from east to west. And in his mercy he has begun to warm the cold hearts of nations at the world's end, as in Kent, which you know through your Queen. Reject idols, their worship, temples, and soothsayers, for God the Father almighty, Jesus Christ his Son, the Holy Spirit, and life everlasting. For idols are helpless, perishable, man-made. [He quotes Psalms 96.5, and 114.4-6.] Destroy them, and accept instead the cross, sign of man's redemption. Accept the words of the preachers, believe, and be baptized, that you may live with God in eternal glory.[2]

[1] II, 9.   [2] II, 10, condensed.

We may note that such preaching was an admirable introduction to the Creed, stressing that now it was widely accepted across the world, and beginning to reach the cold north-west. It includes the traditional attack on 'dead idols', begun in the Old Testament, continued in St Paul's preaching as summarized by himself (I Thess. 1.9, 10), and as illustrated by St Luke (Acts 14.15; 17.29), continued too in the Early Church as all the apologists bear witness.[1] Christians did not follow the Jews in interpreting the second commandment as a complete ban on 'graven images', and made use of painting, mosaic, and sculpture. But they continued the attack on unworthy representations of the divine with the old vehemence. The positive message here is simply, 'Accept the sign of the cross, by which the human race has been redeemed.'

The letter to the Queen takes as its text I Corinthians 7.14, 'The unbelieving husband is sanctified in the wife', and contains this glowing sentence:

> Our heart has leapt for joy at the Lord's bounty to you, in that your witness has kindled a spark of true religion which he may well turn into a flame of love towards him, not only in the mind of your glorious husband, but in that of the whole people who are your subjects.[2]

With St Peter's blessing, he sends 'a mirror of silver and an ivory comb set in gold'. His presents to the King were 'a shirt with one gold ornament, and a cloak from Ankara'. The shirt has sometimes been taken to be a shirt of mail, but *camisa*, like its derivatives, stands for a garment of light material. The present capital of Turkey seems then to have been famous for its wool.

Then came the crisis. Paulinus, perhaps through the Queen, heard about the mysterious stranger, and resolved to challenge the King. Finding him alone, brooding and uncertain still,

> the man of God came up, placed his right hand upon his head, and asked, 'Do you recognize the sign?' He trembled and

---

[1] *After the Apostles*, pages 47-71.   [2] II, 11.

would have fallen at his feet, but Paulinus raised him, and said in a friendly voice, 'From the foes you feared, the Lord gave you escape. The kingdom you desired, by his bounty you have received. Remember the third thing, and do as you promised—accept the Faith and follow his commands'[1]

This was decisive for the King himself, but, for the country, decision must be reached by the Witan. So he summoned his wise men, and bade each in turn to speak. Two of the speeches were notable enough for someone to record, and Bede has preserved them. Coifi, the chief-priest, begins with an impudent reply. He is for hearing the claims of the new religion, for the old one has brought him little profit. He has led in worship of the gods, but they have not given him a leading place in the King's favour. One is left wondering if the chief-priest is scoring a point against the gods, or against the anxious King. The other counsellor goes deeper.

So seems to me, O King, the life of man here on earth, compared with the parts of time beyond our knowledge. When you are seated at dinner with your thanes and ministers in winter time, the hearth fire in the midst, the dining-room made warm, but outside raging blasts of winter rain and snow, there comes a sparrow, flitting swiftly through, in at one window, then out at another. For a moment within, it is safe from the winter's wind, but how short its peace, gone in a moment, from winter to winter back again, out of your sight. So is the life of man. It appears for a space. What comes after, what went before, who rightly knows? If this new teaching brings anything more sure, it seems worth following.[2]

Coifi now asked that the Bishop state the Christian case in detail. Alas, we have no record of Paulinus' words, but we do have Coifi's reaction.

I have long concluded that there is nothing in what we worship, for the more zealously I sought the truth in our religion, the less I found. But now I openly avow that in this preaching there shines that truth which can give us life, salvation, and eternal blessedness. So I say, O King, let the temples and

[1] II, 12.   [2] II, 13.

altars, which we vainly have held as sacred, be forthwith accursed and put to the flames.

Bold talk, but who would do it? So challenged, Coifi was quick to answer. He demanded arms and a stallion—thus breaking at the outset two taboos, for a priest must go unarmed and always ride a mare. With sword and spear 'he rode straight for the idols, the crowd taking him for mad'. The temple was at Goodmanham, eighteen miles east of York (then Godmunddingaham, 'place under the gods' protection', near Weighton, 'sacred enclosure'). He hurled in his spear at the open door, and called on his friends to set the place on fire and destroy it.

Bede continues,

> So King Edwin, with all the nobility of his nation, and most of the people, came to the font, in the eleventh year of his reign, the 627th year of the Lord's incarnation, and about 180 years from the coming of the English. He was baptized at Easter, the twelfth of April.

For all his previous instruction, this was no perfunctory baptism.

> He built a wooden church *while he was being catechized and trained* for receiving baptism. And in this city of York he granted to Paulinus, his teacher and director, an episcopal see.

In marking the beginning of York Minster and of York Diocese, do not overlook the continuing emphasis upon due preparation for meaningful baptism. And as with the King, so it was with the people. At Yeavering, near Wooler,

> for thirty-six days, Paulinus did nothing from morning till night but teach the people, who flocked from every village and place, Christ's word of salvation, and then wash them in the River Glen near by.[1]

Catterick Bridge was the scene of similar baptisms in the Swale. Edwin persuaded Redwald's son, now ruler of the

---

[1] II, 15.

East Angles, to break with heathenism. Paulinus extended his work to Lindsey, and established a Bishop at Lincoln.

Alas! In 633 at Hatfield near Doncaster, King Edwin was killed in battle with the heathen Penda, King of Mercia, and Cadwallon, Christian King of Wales. Paulinus was no faint-heart, but he had come north as chaplain to Ethelburga the bride. With Ethelburga the widow, and the children whom he had baptized, he sadly took ship for Kent, to die ten years later as Bishop of Rochester.[1]

It was under another royal house, and by missionaries of a different tradition, that the Christian cause in Northumbria would be saved.

The power of northern England when Pope Gregory I made his famous puns was Aella, King of Deira. Next came the ascendancy of the rival house of Bernicia, which under Aethelfrith ruled all Northumbria, and sent Aella's son Edwin a fugitive to Redwald, King of the East Anglians. When in 617 Edwin was raised to Northumbria's throne, Oswald, son of Aethelfrith, was similarly exiled. Vague Christian influences over Edwin began during his stay in East Anglia. About Christian influences over Oswald there was nothing vague. He found refuge with the monks of Iona and was then and there converted and baptized. He was the first English King to be deeply Christian in conviction and conduct, destined at his death, in battle against the heathen Penda, to be revered as saint and martyr.

'With an army small, but fortified by faith in Christ', he made a surprise attack upon Cadwallon's vastly superior forces.[2] Like Bede after him, he would find the place-name propitious, Heavenfield, just north of Hexham.

To this day with great reverence the place is shown where he raised the sign of the holy cross. They say that he seized the hastily improvised cross, himself set it in the hole that had

[1] II, 20.
[2] Columba appeared to Oswald in a dream the night before, and promised him victory. Oswald told it in the presence of Adamnan's predecessor as Abbot.

been dug, and with both hands held it upright, while the soldiers filled earth around and planted it. This done, he shouted to the whole army, 'Let us all kneel down and pray to God almighty, the living God and true, that in his mercy he will defend us from a proud and cruel foe. For he knows ours is a righteous warfare to save our country. . . .' Men still cut shavings from that holy cross and put them in water for the sick to drink, or to be sprinkled with, whether men or cattle.[1]

He adds that this became a place of pilgrimage and is rightly honoured

since we find that no sign of the Christian faith, no church, no altar, was set up in any part of Bernicia, before this standard of the holy cross.

Oswald, once on the throne, sent to the Scots among whom he and some of his soldiers had been baptized,

asking them to send some bishop to teach his English subjects the benefits of faith in our Lord, and to give them the sacraments. And soon he got what he asked.[2]

The Abbot of Iona sent first an austere monk, who never won a hearing, and went back to report to his seniors.

I have achieved nothing in teaching the people to whom I was sent. They are uncivilized men, of a hard and barbarous disposition.

So the senior monks called a meeting to see what else they could do.

Aidan had been present when the report was given, and had thus addressed the priest in question. 'It seems to me, Brother, that you were too harsh with your ignorant hearers, and forgot the Apostle's instruction to give them first the milk of simpler doctrine, till little by little, nourished by God's word, they should be able to receive that which is more excellent, and to fulfil God's loftier commands.' All eyes and ears were turned on the speaker at the time. And now when they were discussing his ideas, the thought came home, 'Here is the man

[1] III, 2. [2] III, 3.

to be bishop, and to teach the ignorant and unbelieving, since, above all else, he is full of the grace of discretion, which is mother of all virtues'. And so he was consecrated and sent as missionary. He accepted the mission, and, as at the outset he showed wise discretion, so afterwards he proved himself equipped with many a virtue more.[1]

This sounds promising for our study of missionary method. We shall discuss (1) the base—Lindisfarne, the monastery, and its ways; (2) methods of evangelism—public preaching, dealing with individuals, and village groups; (3) the training of native clergy; (4) the example of the Christian life; (5) the gospel preached.

(1) *The base*. The first strategic decision was Aidan's choice—his and the King's presumably—of a site. It was not to be York, the old Roman headquarters, a British bishopric in 314, Pope Gregory I's choice as centre for a northern mission, Edwin's capital and the see which he gave to Paulinus. Two factors made against this. Aidan came from Iona; and Oswald's chief residence was the rock-fortress of Bamburgh, the Angles' first stronghold on this coast a century before. Now five miles to the north lay Lindisfarne, an island like Iona three miles long, its northern half a narrow sandbank, the southern something like Iona's one-and-a-half-miles in width.

Twice a day the flow of tide surrounds it with waves, an island of the sea, and twice the ebb leaves bare the sands which join it to the coast.[2]

The proper way to visit Lindisfarne still, for all its new concrete causeway over which at low tide you can drive, is barefoot for two miles over the wet sands, the pilgrim way. Bede's point is that Lindisfarne was, as a monastery must be, a place on its own, out of the world; yet wonderfully accessible to, indeed twice a day adjoining, the centre for king and court. He immediately continues,

[1] III, 5.   [2] III, 3.

D

And so the King humbly and willingly gave heed to his advice, and was concerned diligently to build up and extend the Church in his kingdom.

Lindisfarne was reminiscent of Iona, but it was admirably chosen to make the most of an opportunity such as Iona never knew, the King's openness to advice, and zeal in the mission's service. As near to Lindisfarne as Bamburgh, and from Bamburgh only two miles to seaward, is Farne Island, empty except for sea-birds and seals, which became Aidan's favourite retreat. He could face seaward when he needed a monk's alone-ness. He could face the rock-fortress when as a missionary he prayed for this kingdom. This was dramatically illustrated when Penda, heathen King of Mercia, attacked Bamburgh.

> Since he could not take it by battle nor by siege, he tried to burn it. He tore up villages in the countryside, and brought a great collection of beams and rafters, partitions, wattle and thatch, and piled it high round the part of the walls which face inshore. When the wind was favourable, he set it alight, meaning to burn the city.
>
> At this very time, Aidan was staying in Farne Island, two miles away. For he often used to go there for private prayer, or to be quiet. Indeed on the island they will still show you his place of retreat. When he saw smoke and great tongues of fire high over the city walls, he raised his eyes and hands to heaven and exclaimed with tears, 'See, Lord, what evil Penda is doing!' As he said it, the wind changed, and blew the flames back on those who lit them. Many were burnt, all were frightened, and they called off the attack, knowing that the city had the help of God.[1]

The monastic buildings on Lindisfarne were of the simplest, wattle and thatch, like the villages, just mentioned. On Iona they had a church of oak, but not on Lindisfarne, till after Aidan's death in 651 when Abbot Finan built one, 'more suitable to be a cathedral'. But even this was only

[1] III, 16.

roofed with thatch, and had to wait till Abbot Eadbert (687) replaced it with lead.[1]

Other buildings were few. They owned nothing but their cattle. If they received a gift of money, it went straight to the poor, for they needed none. When people of rank came, their purpose was to pray in church, or to hear the Bible expounded, not to be entertained. When the King himself came, with several attendants, if they stayed for a meal, they were content with the plain fare of the monks.[2]

(2) *Methods of evangelism.* Aidan began right away, even before he knew enough English.

> Often one could see the lovely sight of the missionary preaching the gospel, and the King himself interpreting the word of God to thanes and ministers. For in his long exile he had learned the language of the Scots.[3]

Evidently the sort of work which we saw Paulinus doing was taken up again, with the support of more reinforcements than he ever had.

> From then on more Scots missionaries [i.e. from Ireland] began to come, and to preach with great devotion, and those who were priests to baptize the converts. And so churches were built for different places. People gladly came flocking to hear the word. Property was given by the royal bounty, and land for the founding of monasteries, and the English, both little children and those older, were trained by their Scottish teachers to learn and to follow the monastic discipline.

'Churches for different places' implies the beginning of a parish system. 'Founding of monasteries' included some for women. Bede names Heiu, 'the first woman in Northumbria to take vows and the habit of a nun, consecrated by Bishop Aidan.'[4] She was Abbess at Hartlepool. More famous was Hilda, grand-niece of King Edwin and baptized with him. She became a nun in 647, and was given land by Aidan for a small convent on Wearside. She succeeded Heiu at Hartlepool, and then founded and ruled the double monastery (men's and women's), at Whitby. Bede notes that

[1] III, 25.   [2] III, 26.   [3] III, 3.   [4] IV, 23.

the men's section there produced no less than five bishops. Local churches and new monasteries he alike accounts as parts of the Christian occupation of Northumbria.

He gives two pleasing pictures of individual evangelism and of village work. The first shows us Aidan himself on a journey.

> His custom was to travel, whether in town or country, not on horseback but on foot, except when urgency compelled him. This was so that, wherever on his way he came upon any one, rich or poor, he could turn aside. Did they not yet believe? He would invite them to think of Christian baptism. Were they believers? [i.e. from the mission of Paulinus]. Then he would confirm them in the faith and encourage them by word and example to charity and good works. . . . And all who were travelling with him, whether clerical or lay, he would make to meditate—I mean either read the Bible or learn the Psalms. This was his daily task, and that of all his company wherever they went.[1]

Bede gives the second picture as typical of the Lindisfarne tradition.

> Any one dressed as a priest or a monk was sure of respect. Wherever one such appeared, men were glad to receive him as the servant of God. Meeting him on the road, people would run forward, and loved to bow their neck to receive from his hand the sign of the cross, or from his lips a blessing. And they would listen intently to his teaching. But on the Lord's day they would regularly flock to church or monastery to hear the word of God. If a priest chanced to come to a village, the villagers would soon get together, anxious to hear from him the word of life. For priests and other clergy came for nothing else than to preach, baptize, visit the sick, and do other care of souls.[2]

(3) *Training of native clergy.*

At the time of his first coming as Bishop, Aidan received twelve boys of the nation of the English, to be trained in Christ.[3]

[1] III, 5.   [2] III, 26.   [3] III, 26.

In another place, talking of Aidan's giving to the poor all money gifts received, he adds,

> Or sometimes he used to spend them to buy the liberty of those who had been sold as slaves. Many of those so ransomed he took as his pupils, and, when he had brought them to the required standard, ordained them as priests.[1]

Of the first twelve boys mentoned above, some attained great distinction. Eata, Abbot of Melrose by 651, was given rule over Lindisfarne in 664, when the Scots missionaries withdrew, stepping indeed into his master, Aidan's, shoes. Chad that same year became Bishop of York, an Englishman taking, after a break of thirty-one years, the place of Paulinus, first Roman missionary to the north. Chad was later to become first missionary-bishop of Mercia, with Lichfield for his see (667). Chad had three brothers, Cedd, Bishop of the East Saxons (at Tilbury), Cynebil, founder and Abbot of the monastery of Lastingham, and Celin, chaplain to King Aethelwald of Deira. It is possible, though Bede does not say so, that all may belong to the twelve. When in 664 the flow of missionary recruits changed to an ebb-tide back to Ireland, Aidan's foresight had provided experienced native leaders o take their place.

(4) *The example of the Christian life*. Bede begins his account of Aidan by saying two things, that 'he left a most healthy pattern of living to his clergy', and that 'he and those with him commended their doctrine to all men by living just as they taught'. Having continued to Aidan's death in 651, he owns his dislike of Celtic ways, especially with regard to the Easter festival, and adds,

> But as a true historian I have given a straightforward account of the man and his work, praising things praiseworthy, that readers might profit by remembering them. He cared for peace, love, self-control, humility; his spirit triumphed over anger and greed, and despised pride and vainglory. He was

[1] III, 5.

zealous to teach and to do God's will. He knew how to study, and to keep his times of prayer. With true priestly authority he could rebuke the proud and powerful, and with mercy he could comfort the weak, and relieve or defend the poor. To sum up, those who knew him tell us that he took what he knew was taught by the Gospels, the Apostles, and the books of the Prophets, and did his utmost to fulfil them all. These things in him I much admire and love, as surely well-pleasing to God.[1]

From one belonging to the other side of a division, unhappy as any of ours today, this is praise indeed for the noble founder of a noble mission.

(5) *The gospel preached.* Little is said about this, beyond the frequently recurring emphasis on the Bible. But Bede adds to his final paean of praise this doctrinal summary.

About his keeping of Easter, this I do approve, that in his heart he held, and reverenced, and preached, nothing different from ourselves, which is the redemption of mankind, by the passion, resurrection and ascension into heaven, of the Mediator between God and man, himself Man, Jesus Christ.

[1] III, 17.

VI

English Missionaries to the Netherlands and Germany

WILFRID, 678   WILLIBRORD, 690   BONIFACE, 718

THE SUBJECT of English missionaries on the mainland of Europe is for me linked with two ecumenical occasions.

The first was in 1948, when, on my way to the first assembly of the World Council of Churches, I called at Utrecht. At a busy cross-roads near the ancient cathedral, I saw St Willibrord. They had the great granite statue, a monk on a warhorse with a church in his hand, ready for 1940, the 1250th anniversary of his coming. Hitler's blitz that year turned joy into mourning, but after liberation they did not forget. So there he stands. My Dutch friends laughed at my enthusiasm for their patron saint. It was their turn for surprise when I retorted, 'Yours? Why, my grandfather came from the same city of Ripon.' If it is strange that Dutchmen should forget his nationality, it is stranger that Englishmen should never hear his name.

The second occasion was the World Missionary Conference at Willingen in Germany in 1952. On the Sunday which fell in the middle of the gathering, members were invited in groups to different churches, where people from wide areas around came together to receive us. I was fortunate to go to a large village in a countryside which seemed remote from this changing world. Some of the congregation arrived in farm wagons drawn by oxen. Women wore their picturesque dress traditional in that countryside for generations. The minister began to introduce the delegates thus: 'My friends, there are three great events in the history of this village: twelve hundred years ago, when the English missionary St Boniface preached here; four hundred years ago, when Martin Luther left here the German Bible which I hold in my hand; and today, when for the first time in Germany we receive representatives of the worldwide Church'.

One of the greatest glories of English history is the fact that, within the first century of English Christianity, while the country was still a mission-field, it began to become the base from which the rest of northern Europe was to be converted. Let us recall the dates. Missionary work began in Kent in 597. Effective Christian occupation of the north came a generation later, 635. Sussex, the last heathen kingdom, was not entered till 681. Yet as early as 678 an Englishman began missionary work in Frisia, which we now call the Netherlands.

This man is Wilfrid, Abbot of Ripon. He is better known for ending, at the Synod of Whitby, 664, the Celtic mission in England, than for beginning English missions on the mainland of Europe. Let us look at these two developments together. If we use terms current in discussing modern missions, we shall see Wilfrid as the leading figure demanding devolution from foreign (Celtic) mission to indigenous (English) Church, chafing under denominational restrictions imposed by the mission, and demanding a wider ccumenical (which then meant Roman) alignment. But as a Younger Church grows up it needs to become not only self-determining but self-propagating. Even so, we must go on to recognize the same Wilfrid as leader in carrying to northern Europe that missionary zeal which had been the Celtic mission's strongest contribution. Returning from modern terms to Wilfrid's contemporary and biographer, Eddi (Eddius Stephanus), we find him stressing Wilfrid's part in this new mission. He quotes St Paul, 'I laid a foundation and another buildeth thereon' (I Cor. 3.10), and adds,

Wilfrid was the founder, and Willibrord, his product from Ripon, is still engaged in building, with the sweat of much toil, but a reward to all eternity.

The differences between the southern mission, from Rome through Gaul to Kent, and the northern mission, from Ireland through Iona to Lindisfarne, were three, the tonsure, the date of Easter, and church organization.

Celtic monks shaved from the forehead back to a line over the head from ear to ear. The general western usage was to shave the top of the head, leaving a fringe of hair around. But, as an abbot even in this period of controversy wrote,

> Difference of tonsure does no harm to those who have pure faith toward God and true love to their neighbour.

The Irish maintained an older way of calculating Easter, being untouched by a reform of the calendar accepted in Rome in 455. When Christians of the two traditions began to mingle, confusion was inevitable. For example, Oswy, succeeding his brother, King Oswald, in 644, had married Eanfled, the child of King Edwin whom Paulinus had christened in 626, 'firstfruit of the Northumbrian people' (p. 91). From the age of seven she had lived in Kent. Bede says,

> The Queen with her followers kept Easter as in Kent, having a priest from Kent called Romanus, of the catholic persuasion. . . . When the King had ended the Lenten fast and was celebrating Easter, the Queen and her party continued in Lent, being only at Palm Sunday.[1]

But even with regard to this second more serious difficulty, Bede could add,

> As long as Aidan lived, people were prepared to put up with the difference, because everybody loved him so.

Anyone with experience of co-operation between missions of different traditions will agree with this emphasis on personal relations.

From those under his command Wilfrid seems to have won the utmost devotion, but he was better at command than

[1] III, 25.

at co-operation. When King Oswy summoned a Synod at Whitby to consider the Easter question, Wilfrid leapt into the fray with zest, and indeed with something of arrogance.

> Easter as we keep it we have seen in Rome, where the blessed Apostles Peter and Paul lived, taught, suffered, and are buried. So also in Italy, and in Gaul, where we have travelled for study or to pray. And so we find it in Africa, Asia, Egypt, Greece, and all the world, except only for Irish, and Picts, and Britons—two distant islands of the sea, and not even the whole of them, stupidly opposing the whole world.

Colman, the Irish missionary from Iona, Abbot of Lindisfarne, countered Wilfrid's apostolic claim. He supported his reckoning of Easter by the example of the Apostle John, 'who was counted worthy to lean on the Lord's breast'. He was surely quoting Polycrates, Bishop of Ephesus, who in 190 wrote to Victor, Bishop of Rome, about the source of his own Easter tradition.

> In Asia great lights are fallen asleep . . . John who leaned on the Lord's breast. . . .[1]

Colman must have thought—but quite mistakenly—their difference to be a continuation of that which separated Asia Minor from the See of Rome in the early controversy. Wilfrid had his reply, milder now, but decisive.

> Your fathers were holy men. Yet, are those few, in one corner of a distant isle, to take precedence of the universal Church? Your Columba—ours too, since he was Christ's—was a saint and a mighty man. But can you set him against the Prince of the Apostles, to whom the Lord said, 'Thou art Peter, and on this rock I will build my Church, and I will give thee the keys of the kingdom of heaven'?

The King, already more than half-persuaded by his wife, clinched the argument. 'If he be doorkeeper, then I tell you straight, I am not for setting my word against his.'

[1] Eusebius, *Ecclesiastical History*, V, 24.

And so the allegiance of the Church in England was decided. The tradition which had come from Rome through Gaul to Canterbury was to prevail.

The third difference between the two missions concerned organization. This difference is hard to express without making it too defined. Both missions (as we have seen) did establish some local churches; both (as we must have guessed) were generations away from being able to provide a full parish system. But broadly speaking, the southern mission was better equipped to make towards it, and the northern more content to remain monastery-centred, the Abbot and his wandering monks making haphazard pastoral provision for a wide area. Much about this mission appeals to us as simple, spontaneous, and otherworldly. The other tradition might be less impressive in these virtues, but, in a manner typically Roman, it was better organized. It centred all from the start upon the bishop, a policy which presumed the diocese; then, as the work grew, a number of dioceses; and so a province. Again to translate into modern terms, one sees a similar contrast between those missions which stand for widespread evangelism, and those which from the outset have more regard for the church as an institution.

Then as now, in order to conserve the results of simple evangelism, one might need to leave simplicity behind; be less spontaneous and more given to planning; and as for otherworldliness, in those days one might have to haggle with a king, or with a feudal lord, to get a bishopric endowed, or provision for a local church. The decision at Whitby, though none of this was mentioned, was to affect not only England, but missions from England to the Continent. Missionaries would go, as Augustine and his Benedictines had come, with something of a thought-out plan, and would follow it, looking where Augustine had looked for direction, though few Popes could be expected to compare with Gregory the Great as 'Servant of the servants of God'. That is how Willibrord became Apostle of the Netherlands, and Boniface the Apostle of Germany.

When two rivers flow together, the distinctive colour of the one water may be lost, but the river itself continues in the added depth and the stronger flow. The Church which was to send missionaries to Europe was formed by the confluence of the two missions. Though on the surface all may seem to belong to Rome there are depths where we shall recognize the contribution from the Celtic stream. Especially is this so in the case of Willibrord, who was himself a Northumbrian.

In Wilfrid the Celtic characteristics—simple, spontaneous, and otherworldly—may seem hard to find. He was born in 634, the son of a Northumbrian thane. An unkind stepmother caused him to leave home at the age of thirteen and turn up at King Oswy's court. The Queen, Eanfled, was interested in this handsome boy and his desire for the Church's service. A friend of the King's, afflicted with paralysis, had decided to retire to Lindisfarne, and the Queen recommended Wilfrid as his attendant. At Lindisfarne he first learned the ways of monks, and learned the Psalter by heart, as a monk should. This was in Aidan's time; did he catch anything from the saint? Queen Eanfled's patronage again gave him an introduction to her cousin, the King of Kent. And here in 653, aged 19, he met another young Northumbrian noble who had taken to religion, Benedict Biscop, later to found at Wearmouth and Jarrow the monasteries which became the lifelong home of the great Bede himself. The two youths travelled together by way of Lyons to Rome, and the glory of Lyons and its history held Wilfrid even longer than did Rome. He returned to Northumbria in 658, to become Abbot at Ripon in 661, the outstanding figure at Whitby in 664, Bishop in 665. Of his forty-five years as Bishop half was spent in exile, from 678 to 686 because he fell foul of both Egfrid his King and Theodore his Primate; and from 691 to 705 because he opposed the needful division of Northumbria into several sees, and demanded that it should remain ecclesiastically one, and his. Eddi, his biographer, elaborately defends his cause and details his appeals to the Pope, and the Pope's decisions. Bede recounts the facts somewhat wearily and adds, 'And so for his four remaining years [705-9], he led his life in peace.'[1] Like Eddi, Bede claims him as England's first missionary.

> Expelled from his See [in 678], he took ship to go to Rome to plead his cause with the Pope, but a strong wind drove him to Frisia. . . . He was the first to begin there the work of evangelism which later that most reverend Bishop of Christ, Willibrord, fulfilled with great devotion.

Bede in another place gives an account, far longer than that of Eddi, of Wilfrid's missionary work in Sussex, 'till then in heathen bondage'. He must have got it from his friend Acca, in his youth companion of Wilfrid's exile, and for twenty-three years (709-32) his successor as Bishop at Hexham. 'Though the King's displeasure shut him out of his own country and diocese, there was no keeping him from the ministry of the Gospel.'[2] Bede knew that here one sees Wilfrid at his Christian best.

What then do we see of his missionary methods? Eddi tells us more than Bede about Frisia. Wilfrid

> found there crowds of heathen. He was honourably received by Aldgisil their king. Our holy priest, with the king's permission, preached the word of God daily.

English and Dutch languages may then have been sufficiently alike for him to need no interpreter. The content of the preaching, as Eddi reports (or guesses) it, is merely a summary of the Creed. Most of the chiefs, he says, and many thousands of the people, were baptized, a success due to unusually large catches of fish, and unusually good harvests of every kind. These were taken as signs of blessing from the God whom Wilfrid preached.

[1] V, 19.   [2] IV, 13.

This of course may have been God's method, but we can hardly give Wilfrid the credit. However, the catch of fish does seem to link with later happenings in pagan Sussex. Bede says that here the King and Queen were favourable, the King converted by the King of Mercia, who acted as sponsor at his baptism, the Queen Christian born in the country of the Hwicci (Worcestershire and Gloucestershire). Five or six monks were already settled in a small Irish monastery at Bosham, but with little influence. For three years there had been drought and famine, with frequent suicides among despairing people. On the day of Wilfrid's first baptisms rain fell—again a sign of God's blessing. But Wilfrid himself had something to add. Perhaps remembering the harvest of the sea, which they had put first in Frisia, he found that in Sussex, even in times of famine, the people knew nothing of fishing, apart from netting eels. So he set his men to collect eel nets, and joining them together, they were soon able to give thanks for a catch of 300 fishes, and the demonstration of a new industry. Bede says of this Christian social concern,

> By this kindness the Bishop turned the hearts of all to love him, and they were the readier to listen to his preaching about hopes of heaven, since he had ministered to their temporal needs.[1]

The King gave him and his following lands for a monastery in Selsey, and he settled there as Bishop for five years, instructing and baptizing all belonging to the estates, including serfs to the number of 250, both men and women, to whom with baptism he gave their freedom.

We must now turn to Willibrord. Alcuin, his kinsman, who was to become from 782 onwards leader of the Renaissance of learning at Charlemagne's court, wrote a *Life of Willibrord*. Far from being that scholar's most distinguished work, it is brief and full of miracle stories. Bede, Willi-

[1] IV, 13.

brord's admiring contemporary, and friend of Acca, who, with Wilfrid, went out to Frisia to see the missionary at work, adds much to our knowledge of him.

Willibrord was born in 658. Alcuin says that his father, Wilgils, 'as soon as the child was weaned, gave him to the monks at Ripon'. Later Wilgils became a hermit on the north bank of the Humber near its mouth, and dedicated his chapel, soon to develop into a small monastery, to St Andrew. This looks like a memory, from the days of Paulinus, Bishop of York, of that St Andrew's monastery in Rome which was the source of the mission. Wilgils' monastery, Alcuin says, by the time he wrote, he had himself come to inherit. With the father a hermit, and the child given to the Ripon monks, we may guess that the mother had died. A monastery seems a strange place for a baby, away from woman's care. But as the child grew, it would in one respect be a wonderful place, the only place where there were books, and men who could read them, and Latin which was the key to learning.

As a little boy he must have watched the building of Ripon's first minster. Eddi describes it as

a church which, from foundation to roof, was built of polished stone, and supported by various pillars and colonnades.

Perhaps some of the pillars were Roman, and came from Aldborough (Roman Isurium), seven miles away. The Northmen would destroy everything above ground, but Wilfrid's crypt remains. With that at Hexham, a church dedicated to St Andrew[1] and built by Wilfrid, it is all that remains of the work of this great church-builder.

There was another sight for the boy to remember when the minster was consecrated. King Egfrid was there with his brother and many nobles. The dedication was to Peter, Prince of the Apostles. And imposing as a prince himself, Wilfrid the Abbot stood before the altar which was decked with purple and cloth of gold. On it were Wilfrid's gifts to

[1] Another memory of the source of the Roman mission.

his church, a great gold cross, and another gift of which Eddi speaks with wonder:

> a marvellous ornament for the house of God, unheard of before our time, the four Gospels on purpled vellum in letters of gold, and illuminated, with a case of pure gold set with precious stones.

Did the boy, one wonders, ever hear the Abbot tell (as Eddi did, for he retells it) of visiting in his own youth the monastery of St Andrew in Rome, founded by Pope Gregory the Great, and from which Augustine and Paulinus came? In the chapel there he had seen

> the four Gospels, set over the top of the altar. And he humbly knelt and prayed the Lord to grant him ability to read, and eloquence to teach, those same Gospels among the nations.

In his gift to Ripon minster Wilfrid was surely remembering. And when in 678 he found himself among the heathen of Frisia, he remembered again in a different way, and found his prayer answered. That Ripon monastery was to contribute to the spread of the Gospel 'among the nations'.

In that same year, 678, Willibrord, now a monk aged twenty, left Ripon for Ireland. Wilfrid and Benedict Biscop in their youth had gone to Rome, but Ireland, source of the other mission, had long attracted Northumbria's youth, whether in quest of greater learning or of greater holiness. Egbert was such a one, of noble birth, who had gone about 660.[1] Plague struck the monastery at which he lived, and he thought that his hour had come. He vowed that if God would spare his life he would renounce his homeland (that familiar Celtic idea of 'pilgrimage'), keep one day and night's complete fast every week, and recite the entire Psalter every day. He was spared, so he stayed on, becoming an Abbot famous even among Irish monks for holiness and learning. The place was called Rathmelsigi, and may be Mellifont near Drogheda in County Louth. Bede says that in spite of these and other austerities he lived

[1] Bede, III, 27.

to be ninety. Willibrord went to Egbert and stayed with him for twelve years. In the latter part of this period Egbert began to plan

> the work of an apostle to those nations in Germany from whom the Anglo-Saxons are known to have sprung.[1]

Did Willibrord know of Wilfrid's work there, and tell him? Or was it just chance that Willibrord's former and present abbots should be concerned with missions in the one place? Egbert may well have said to himself (like Columba, turning 'pilgrimage' into mission), 'Why renounce one's homeland merely to sit in Christian Ireland, when over the narrow seas there is work to do among the heathen?' This was the nearest heathen land, and these were, even as he said, the Anglo-Saxons' kindred. So he chose as his colleagues 'the most vigorous men and good preachers', and got ready all that was necessary for their journey. What happened is best described in the graphic account by Bede.

> One of his monks, formerly of Melrose when Boisil was Abbot, came to Egbert early one morning and said, 'After matins I lay down again and slept, and my dear old master who brought me up came to me and said, "Do you recognize me?" "Yes", I said, "you are Boisil." "For this," he said, "I am come, to bring our Lord and Saviour's reply to Egbert, and yet it rests with you to take it to him. Tell him that he must not make the journey that he has planned. God's will is that he should go to Columba's monasteries to instruct them rather." '
>
> Egbert received the message, but he said, 'Tell no one else, lest it be mere illusion', though he was afraid that it might be true. But he wanted to go on preparing. . . .
>
> A few days afterwards, this brother told him that after matins Boisil had appeared again, and said, 'Why so lukewarm your report? Go now and tell him, Whether you want or not, to Columba's monks you shall go, because they do not plough a straight furrow.'[2]

[1] V, 9.   [2] He did later persuade the Iona monks to conform.

Again Egbert said, 'Do not make it public.' He could no longer doubt, yet he tried to go on, laying aboard stores for a long journey, and waiting some days for a fair wind. There came one night a savage storm, destroyed most of the ship's gear, washed the ship aground, though all that belonged to Egbert and his party was saved. Then said he, with the prophet Jonah, 'For my sake this great tempest is upon us' (Jonah 1.12). He changed his plans and stayed.[1]

One of his men, Witbert, did go to Frisia, but there was a new king since Wilfrid's time, and after two years Witbert returned in despair.

Egbert kept on with the idea of sending holy and industrious men for the work of the Word, and among them one outshone the rest, as presbyter, and man of worth—Willibrord.[2]

And so the call came to him, and in 690 he sailed with eleven others. As so often, twelve seemed the right number for a mission.

Alcuin, his kinsman, leaves this little pen-picture of him,

Bright with every excellence, well proportioned in body, honourable in appearance, handsome of face, glad of heart, wise in counsel, delightful in conversation, composed in manner, and strenuous in all the work of God.

Bede writes in 731,

Willibrord is still alive, in venerable old age, a Bishop now for 36 years. Countless the spiritual battles he has fought! And now with all his heart he sighs for his reward on high.[3]

He still had nine years to go, dying at the age of eighty-two. His missionary service had lasted fifty years.

If Willibrord's religious background was a blend of northern Celtic and southern Roman traditions, so at least in its origins was the Christianity of Wessex which produced Winfrith, whose episcopal name was

---

[1] V, 9.   [2] V, 10.   [3] V, 11.

to be Boniface. The missionary to Wessex was Birinus, commissioned in 633 by Pope Honorius I, apparently without reference to Canterbury. The contribution from the north was made by Oswald, baptized in Iona, in 633 newly become King of Northumbria, and soon to summon missionaries to Lindisfarne. He was in Wessex as suitor for the hand of the daughter of Cynegils the King. Powerful advocate of the faith as he always was, Oswald was probably the chief influence in bringing Cynegils to baptism, the son-in-law-to-be acting as godfather. Bede calls Oswald's later co-operation with Aidan, as interpreter, a 'lovely sight', and here he uses the word again, 'a most lovely relationship, worthy of God',[1] The two Kings established Birinus in his See of Dorchester (nine miles south of Oxford), where, says Bede, 'he built and dedicated many churches, and called many populations to the Lord'.

Winfrith was born about 679, probably, though the claim is late, at Crediton, into a family connected with Wessex royalty. Already in childhood called to be a monk, he went for schooling to a monastery at Exeter, and then to another at Nursling, near Winchester. Here Abbot Winbert inspired him with a love of learning. He was used as teacher of his fellow monks, in Latin grammar and style, both prose and verse, in the Bible and in its exposition. Even as a missionary he tried to keep up with this, and wrote to monks at Jarrow for

> works of that biblical scholar Bede, who has lately lit such a candle of the Church among you,

and to Egbert, Archbishop of York, for

> anything Bede writes, especially his sermons for the Church year, which would be a useful manual for our preaching, and his commentary on the Proverbs.

One of his late letters is to the Bishop of Winchester for a commentary on six of the Prophets by Winbert, his old teacher, 'but in big letters, now that my old eyes cannot see

[1] III, 7.

small-lettered manuscripts'. Still under forty, he had been
entrusted with delicate negotiations with the authorities at
Canterbury, was widely known as a coming leader, and at
Nursling talked of as the next Abbot. Then he turned
his back on a promising career. He was of a vigorous,
adventurous disposition. But it was more than love of
adventure; it was the call of God. He must go off to Willibrord in his dangerous work as a missionary in the Netherlands. After a false start in 716—a rising of Frisia against
the Franks made his stay impossible—he went out in 718.
Willibrord wanted to keep him as colleague, and successor,
in Utrecht. But after learning his job he pushed eastward
into Germany.

Beside the short *Life of Boniface* written before 768
by Willibald, one of his English missionary-priests, gathering
his material from eye-witnesses, letters to and from Boniface have come down to us, carefully preserved in his
favourite monastery of Fulda. These are thus summarized
by Othlon, about the year 1100:

> They show with what respect he was received by the Pope,
> and how he sent him to preach to all the German peoples,
> with what toil he brought Germany to the feet of Christ,
> and rescued it not only from pagans and heretics, but also
> from false Christians and depraved priests, as it were from
> ravening wolves.

In the case of Patrick, we judged his leaving Britain to
take him beyond the scope of this book, contenting ourselves
with just such a summary of his mission (p. 43). With
Willibrord and Boniface we must glance at policy, motive,
and method, for much of what they did they had learned
in Britain, itself so recently a mission-field. We must notice
the following:

1. *A developed policy, working towards dioceses, in a
   Province, all under the direction of the Pope*

This policy has dimmed their lustre with some English
church historians, who suspected extension of papal author-

ity, even before the Reformation, and even when it was on the side of the angels. Of Willibrord in 691, Bede says,

> As soon as he knew that he had permission [from Pippin II] to preach in Frisia, he hastened to Rome, that his mission might be with the blessing and licence of Pope Sergius.[1]

This was the beginning of a link with the Pope which was to be maintained and strengthened, and a view of the Pope's authority strange to most of Western Europe at this time, but henceforth to endure in theory, and often to be made good in practice. Pope Leo I had talked in this way from the centre. It was even more important that English missionaries should be acting in this way on the expanding frontiers of Christendom.

In 695 Pippin asked Willibrord to go to Rome again, and Alcuin says,

> The Pope consecrated him publicly in true apostolic fashion, with great solemnity, as Archbishop. . . . He gave him the name of Clement, and invested him with his robes, including the sacred pallium.

Boniface was the devoted, and always obedient, servant of four successive Popes. His first act in 718 was to go for the Pope's commission. After service in Saxony and Hesse, he reported his success, with thousands of baptisms, and was invited to Rome where he was consecrated Bishop, with an oath of loyalty which only bishops in and around Rome itself till then had taken. In 739 the Pope wrote to him about

> a hundred thousand of the German people, loosed from pagan bonds and gathered into the Church through your efforts and those of Prince Charles.

Boniface planned further work among the Saxons of the north, but the Pope turned him to reorganization and reform of the Church in Bavaria, then in Hesse and Thuringia, and from 741 among the Franks themselves. Only with his

[1] V, 11.

retirement from the great See of Mainz in 753 was the aged saint able to resume his missionary calling.

The fact that Pope Gregory the Great had himself established in England a new Province, with an Archbishop of his appointment, led English missionaries in the expanding domain of the Franks to extend this system, assuming for the Pope a like central directing power, and for each part a similar provincial and metropolitan organization. At a time when Syria, Palestine, Egypt and North Africa, strongholds of the Early Church, were overrun by triumphant Islam; when south-east Europe was threatened by heathen Slavs; and Italy itself was insecure because of Arian Lombards; England contributed decisively to the survival and recovery of the Church, not only by further missionary expansion, but by stress upon the Church's unity, and by expressing that unity in obedience to Rome, in following Roman standards of organization, of liturgy (the Gregorian Sacramentary), and of monastic discipline (the Benedictine Rule).

In contrast to all this, we must also notice:

2. *A simple missionary motive—concern for men*

Missionaries of this last generation have shrunk from the element of truth in anti-Christian propaganda, associating Christian missions with the colonial and imperial interests of Great Powers. In 1947 Indian independence brought in one land of the Younger Churches deliverance from this embarrassment. In 1949 this judgement brought the end of China Missions. But from St Paul's claim to Roman citizenship onwards, empires have served the cause of Christian expansion. In the seventh century the Franks were extending their power eastwards back towards their original German home. The attitude of Pippin and his son Charles Martel was not that of foreigners come to conquer, but of kinsmen who return to civilize. In 687 they reached the part of Frisia centred upon Utrecht. In 690 Willibrord went out. He may, or may not, have known. In 722 when Boniface pushed east, so had the conquering Franks. The cause of

Frankish imperialism was their opportunity, but it was not their motive.

Nor must we read the above paragraph about extension of papal authority as though this were a kind of spiritual imperialism. Such words might be used by some to describe their policy, but it was not their motive. Bede's last picture of the aged Willibrord (p. 114) is as simple as that in the New Testament of one who has fought the good fight, finished the course, kept the faith, and looks for the crown (II Tim. 3.7). In 738 defeat of the Old Saxons by Charles Martel seemed to open the way for the winning of the closest kin of the English. Boniface wrote to England,

> To all bishops, priests, deacons, canons, clerks, abbots, abbesses, monks, nuns, and all who fear God. Remember us in your prayers. . . . Pray that God and our Lord Jesus Christ . . . may turn their hearts to the faith . . . and join them to the family of Mother Church. . . . Pity them, for their cry is, We are of one blood with you.

Deep concern for men—that is the simplest and the purest of missionary motives.

With regard to 1 and 2 above, we had better guard against two misunderstandings. First, Englishmen, while loyal to prince and Pope, were not subservient to either. One letter of Boniface's in 746 was sent to Ethelbald, King of Mercia, seven of his English missionary-bishops adding their signatures. They assure him of their joy in his prosperity and their prayers for his good. But they have heard grave charges—that the King is living in adultery, and has even violated nuns.

> If a slave who takes his master's wife commits a hideous crime, what of a man who befouls with his lust the bride of Christ?

They add that even the heathen in Germany have a right instinct about sexual morality. If English people live, as even the heathen are saying, in open immorality, we shall become degenerate and degraded, like other nations before us. We have another letter of 742, in which Boniface says bluntly,

> If your Holiness would put an end to heathen customs which survive in Rome, . . . it would help us in teaching the Christian faith to heathen here.

And second, princely patronage and papal authority did not save missionaries from all danger. There is a shrine in the church of St Cunibert, Cologne, to two Englishmen called Hewald, who came when Willibrord did, killed, one with a sword thrust, the other by slow torture. On Walcheren island Willibrord forgave a heathen priest whose murderous slash with his sword only just missed him. One of Boniface's recruits from Glastonbury wrote back to the monastery,

> Our work is not in vain in the Lord, but it is dangerous and hard, subject to hunger, thirst and cold, with attacks from the heathen. Pray for us power to speak, and to endure in the work and see fruits for our labours.

A letter in 755, the last year of Boniface's life, speaks of thirty churches and monasteries burned. And it was 'attacks from the heathen' which killed him.

3. *Method*

Things done in Britain tended to recur in Germany, sometimes because they were known and consciously repeated, but often because they belonged to general missionary practice, or met similar needs.

One striking feature of this mission is the prominence of women. This can hardly be unrelated to the beginning of the Roman mission to England (p. 81), and developments of the Celtic mission under Aidan (p. 99). In Wessex Boniface seems to have had nuns as well as monks among his pupils, and as a missionary he had many among his correspondents. They write for his advice, try to get books which he wants, send him an altar cloth or some clothing, and all undertake to pray for his mission. The earliest such letter which we have is from Leoba in 732, a nun at Wimborne. She tells him he is a friend of her father, and kinsman of her mother, and she, though all unworthy, thinks of him as brother. She asks him to correct for her a Latin verse. Naughty little nun, she so much wanted to impress, that she copied it from an instruction book by Aldhelm.[1] This letter is the beginning of a flow of concern for the mission from English nunneries and monasteries, and a flow of recruits. In 746 Boniface wrote to the Abbess Cuniberga, sister of the King of Wessex, who ruled this double monastery[2] of Wimborne, asking for their prayers.

> Pray for me, lest I, the last and least sent out to preach the gospel, should have no fruit for my labours, should pass away without spiritual children; and lest some whom I had accounted sheep on Christ's right hand, should turn out to be stinking butting goats upon his left.

A number of distinguished sisters came out in 748, including Leoba, who became Abbess at Bischofsheim. Of such recruits from English monasteries, how many were there? In 753, knowing that his course was almost run, Boniface wrote to King Pippin.

> Continue to support my disciples after my death, for they are almost all foreigners, some priests in local churches, some monks, some young boys in training, some grown old in this mission with me.

We know the names of only a handful, or rather two handfuls, for we know just about the same number of women as of men. There must have been scores. There may have been hundreds. Few periods and few places have seen women take so large a part in the work of the Church. There is a parallel in the modern period, when foreign missionary work has again opened to women their most responsible

---

[1] G. F. Browne, *Boniface and His Companions*, p. 71.
[2] I.e. monastery and nunnery, like Hilda's at Whitby (p. 99).

sphere, and proved a task which, without women as partners, men could hot have done.

Willibrord made one expedition by sea to Schleswig, territory of a Danish king 'savage as a wild beast, and hard as a stone'. He was able to bring back thirty boys—like Aidan's school of twelve English boys at Lindisfarne (p. 100)—hoping to train them as missionaries to their own people.

Most that we hear of preaching is a repetition of the conventional attack on false gods, who are really devils, and the call to forsake the errors of their fathers for the truth. However, one letter to Boniface, from his faithful, and thoughtful, friend, Daniel, Bishop of Winchester, suggests a more sympathetic approach. J. T. Addison in *The Medieval Missionary* suggests that this smacks of 'the intellectual argumentation of the student' rather than the active evangelist. But Winchester was part of a young Church then, with plenty of heathen and half-heathen to preach to. And Sussex, entirely pagan until Daniel's own lifetime, lay bordering on his territory. The following is a free rendering of his advice.

> Do not begin by attacking what they claim as to the origin of their gods, but rather ask, Was it through the intercourse of parents? Is not that more human than divine?
>
> If they were born, they had a beginning, and did not exist before. Then has the universe a beginning? If so, who made it? If not, who ruled it before there were gods?
>
> Where did the first god come from? Do gods and goddesses still have children? If not, why not? If so, however many are there going to be?

In all this the point is to set questions going for which there is only the Christian answer—surely sound educational method.

> Who is the strongest god, and most to be feared?
> What do the gods give, goods of this life, or a future and

eternal reward? If this life, then are Christians less blessed? Look and see!

What good are sacrifices? Do the gods need them, or men decide to give them? If they need, why cannot they as gods help themselves? If they do not, why offer useless sacrifice?

These questions, and others like them, bring up calmly and with moderation, not in an irritating and offensive manner. And here and there you may slip in a comparison with our belief. And so they will be, not annoyed, but somewhat ashamed of their crude ideas.

Suggest also that, if gods are powerful and just, they must not only reward their worshippers, but punish those who despise them. Do they—when the Christians turn the whole world from their worship and overthrow their idols? The Christians prosper in fertile lands, with wine and olives and many good things, leaving to the heathen and their gods only the frozen lands.

Keep reminding them of the supremacy of the Christian world, and that, in comparison, few persist in the old superstitions. Tell them that once the whole world was given up to idolatry, till illumined by the grace of Christ, and knowledge of the one true God, it was brought to life and reconciled to God.

We may hesitate before this last appeal to Christian success, but missionary expansion has almost always been by influence from a higher civilization, *downwards*. In these days we need to be reminded, in spite of our healthy reaction against all feelings of superiority, that not only the Christian message, and the individual Christian life, but a Christian society and a Christian nation do contribute to the furtherance of the gospel.

Sometimes a missionary would see that the old faiths were tottering, and that one bold action might bring them down. It was so with Willibrord at a sacred spring in Heligoland. For generations folk had come to draw water, but in silence, not daring to speak a word, so sacred was the place. Willibrord brought his converts there, took them with him into the pool, shouted for all to hear, 'I baptize thee in the name of the Father. . . .' And nothing happened, so the old god must have slunk away. This is closely parallel to one action of Columba's (p. 65).

Such also was the chance which Boniface recognized at the oak of Geismar. The oak tree stood, like ancient superstition itself, deep-rooted in the past. Men said that for hundreds of years it had been sacred to Thor, the god of thunder. It might stand another hundred years—unless a man decided to hew it down. Boniface decided, and told the people so. From miles around they gathered, hardly believing he would dare. They kept their distance to be safe when the lightning should flash and consume him. In awful silence they watched the Bishop strip to the waist, heard the thud of his axe as it fell with regular strokes on the base of the tree. Had he struck some hidden weakness? Instead of the lightning flash, there came a sudden wind, and the old oak crashed down and broke into four pieces. He called now for others to come, had the timbers shaped, and of the pagan oak tree built a Christian chapel—a sign of the downfall of paganism in all Central Germany.

Boniface's concern for evangelism finds its crowning illustration in the events which led to his martyrdom. At the age of seventy-four he retired from the Archbishopric of Mainz. What he sought was not, as did so many monks, to retreat into solitude. For fourteen years his chief task —not of his choice but at the Pope's bidding—had been rule, administration, and reform. He longed to end as he had begun, a simple missionary among the heathen of the Netherlands. It was there on June 5th, Whitsun Eve, that the end came. He had been on a preaching tour, won converts, instructed and baptized them. They were to meet him that day for confirmation. A band of armed men attacked his camp. He called to his companions not to defend him. Long afterwards, an old woman told that as a girl she had been there waiting to be confirmed. She had seen the old Bishop hold up a book he had been reading, to guard his head as a sword came crashing down. Among the relics at the shrine of St Boniface in the minster at Fulda is a book with blood stains and a sword cut deep through a hundred-and-forty parchment pages. If this were a Gospel or a Massbook, we might doubt if it were genuine. But the contents of the book so exactly fit the time and the occasion. It contains, among other writings, two by St Ambrose of Milan, three hundred years before, one on 'The Holy Spirit', and the other called 'How good it is to die'. It was Whitsun Eve and he had been reading the first to be ready for his confirmations. He was seventy-five, and had been reading the second, also to be ready. For this last act, he had brought no pattern from Britain, for there among the missionaries, both northern Celtic and southern from Rome, there had not been a single martyr. But he had his Pattern, and the testimony, sealed with his blood, was testimony to Christ.

The Netherlands and Germany are really the beginning of the story, not its end. Go on to about the year 1000, and you will find a Viking chief, Olaf Trygvassen, coming to Britain to rob and burn and kill, and being baptized by a hermit in the Scilly Isles, confirmed by the Bishop of Winchester, and returning as Norway's first Christian King; and Cnut, who ruled as a Christian in England first, becoming heir to Denmark's throne. Willibrord, we saw, once began training thirty Danish boys for work farther north than he could go. All the Scandinavian countries were helped towards the light by a long succession of English missionaries.

From so unexpected a quarter came the conversion of all North Europe.

BOOKS FOR FURTHER READING

Bede: A History of the English Church and People, Leo Sherley-Price, Penguin Classics. A lively modern translation.

Bede, Latin text with English opposite, 2 vols in Loeb Classical Library.

St Patrick, his Writings and Life, N. J. D. White. SPCK. Includes Patrick's Confession and Letter, and Muirchu's Memoir.

Libri Sancti Patricii, Latin text in 'Texts for Students' IV, SPCK.

Adomnan's Life of Columba, A. O. and M. O. Anderson, Nelson. Latin text, translation, introduction and notes.

The Anglo-Saxon Missionaries in Germany, C. H. Talbot, Sheed and Ward. Gives Alcuin's Life of Willibrord, Willibald's Life of Boniface, and the best of Boniface's correspondence, in English.

Boniface of Crediton and his Companions, G. F. Browne, SPCK, 1910. Excellent commentary on the letters.

The Church in Anglo-Saxon England, John Godfrey, Cambridge, 1962. An attractive and accomplished history.

Early English Church History, William Bright, Oxford, 1887. Still a standard work.

The Medieval Missionary, J. T. Addison, International Missionary Council, 1936. Most useful, but limited edition and long out of print.

Some other books are mentioned in the text of the book or footnotes.

Progress beyond this list might well take directions from Godfrey's full bibliography (above).

INDEX